T0145690

PRAISE FOR
BRANDON BRITTINGHAM AND
CONVERTING UNITS TO DOLLARS

As a coach and consultant for the Elite CEOs and Team Leaders, you come across a select few who bring something dramatically different from the rest. Brandon Brittingham is that operator and as in all things he does, his property management program will dramatically impact the landscape of your business.

- Jon Cheplak

Looking to grow a property management company and for a no-fluff book that gives you actionable steps to really scale a company? I took away so many actionable steps that will improve my business—100 percent this book is the right resource for you.

- Carl SanFilippo, REMAX First & Tri County, New Jersey

I've been in the property management business for a couple of years and was building it super slowly, the best that we knew. With this book, you're going to learn how to scale your business by building it properly from day one and having the right divisions and departments online, the systems, the contracts—hey, even how to acquire business. This is the next pillar of business.

- Ron Wysocarski, CEO at Wyse Home Team Realty

This book is straight up the bomb! Seriously, amazing content and I'm excited to build out my property management business because of it!

- Kevin Kauffman, The Group 46:10 Real Estate Network

CONVERTING
UNITS TO
DOLLARS

BRANDON BRITTINGHAM

CONVERTING UNITS TO DOLLARS

ELITE OPTS PROPERTY MANAGEMENT

Advantage

Published by Advantage, Charleston, South Carolina.
Member of Advantage Media Group.

ADVANTAGE is a registered trademark, and the Advantage colophon is a trademark of Advantage Media Group, Inc.

Printed in the United States of America.

10 9 8 7 6 5 4 3 2 1

ISBN: 978-1-64225-266-8
LCCN: 2021920582

Cover design by George Stevens.
Layout design by David Taylor.

This publication is designed to provide accurate and authoritative information in regard to the subject matter covered. It is sold with the understanding that the publisher is not engaged in rendering legal, accounting, or other professional services. If legal advice or other expert assistance is required, the services of a competent professional person should be sought.

Advantage Media Group is proud to be a part of the Tree Neutral® program. Tree Neutral offsets the number of trees consumed in the production and printing of this book by taking proactive steps such as planting trees in direct proportion to the number of trees used to print books. To learn more about Tree Neutral, please visit **www.treeneutral.com**.

Advantage Media Group is a publisher of business, self-improvement, and professional development books and online learning. We help entrepreneurs, business leaders, and professionals share their Stories, Passion, and Knowledge to help others Learn & Grow. Do you have a manuscript or book idea that you would like us to consider for publishing? Please visit **advantagefamily.com**.

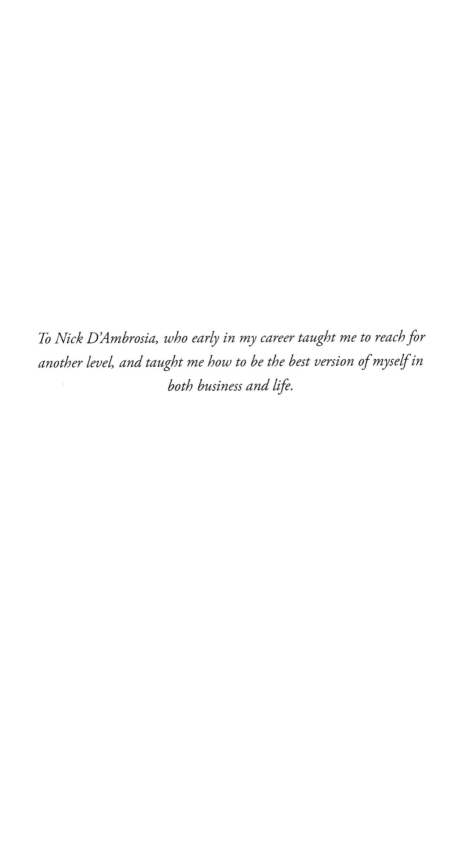

To Nick D'Ambrosia, who early in my career taught me to reach for another level, and taught me how to be the best version of myself in both business and life.

THE SUBJECT MATTER IN THIS BOOK IS NOT
INTENDED TO BE LEGAL OR TAX ADVICE BUT
RATHER A GUIDE. CONSULT WITH AN ATTORNEY
OR CPA ON ALL LEGAL AND TAX MATTERS.

CONTENTS

PREFACE

Real estate is changing. The consumer expects more. Companies like Amazon and Apple creating an ecosystem of products and convenience have changed the consumer's mindset. Companies like Uber have changed the consumers mindset on speed. Airbnb has changed how people travel—the list goes on and on.

If you do not adapt your business to the wants and needs of the consumer, you will be out of business. In the end, the consumer always wins.

The real estate transaction is progressing more and more to the consumers' demands of solving all their problems. I figured this out years ago. If the consumer has to go somewhere else for a particular silo of a real estate need, you may lose them forever.

There is a tech arms race going after the consumer in the real estate transaction and the tech companies are building it around handling all parts of the real estate transaction.

Commission income can also be an up and down rollercoaster. Years ago, with these two things in mind, I pursued building a property management business.

Now, handling all parts of the real estate transaction is all the rage. Property management ties to so many parts of a real estate transaction—both now and in the future—creates wealth, and opens you up to a whole other lane of buyers and sellers.

Many people shy away from this part of the transaction, while others in the market pursue it and take market share.

The real estate world is at a crossroads. Adapt or die. That's what I did, and it's why my companies are thriving.

FOR MORE TRAINING AND INFORMATION ON THIS COURSE VISIT BRANDONSBRAIN.ORG

CHAPTER 1

THE PROS OF PROPERTY MANAGEMENT

If you don't make money while you sleep, you'll
work till the day that you die.
—WARREN BUFFETT

"How do we create residual income?" That was the big question my team members and I asked ourselves as we began each day facing one of the tough realities of real estate sales: no hustle, no commissions.

I'd come to that painful realization years earlier, after my first great year in sales. I'd conducted around 150 transactions myself, and as I reflected on my success during the holiday season, it hit me: come January 1, I'd have to start all over again—and there were no guarantees that I'd do as well as I had going forward.

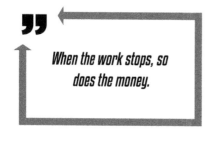

When the work stops, so does the money.

Building predictable income in real estate sales is possible, but it takes a lot of time, serious skill, and—of course—a willingness to keep grinding year after year. When the work stops, so does the money.

But that's not the case with *residual income*. Regardless of what you call it—"mailbox money" or "money earned while sleeping," for instance—residual income is cash that arrives regularly without an everyday hustle, like the one required to earn sales commissions in the real estate business.

And for many, having residual income means just what Mr. Buffett said: you won't have to work until your last breath.

With that in mind, I knew that, eventually, I'd have to think less like a real estate agent and more like an investor—identifying and making transactions that would continue to pay long after the deals were complete.

Fast-forward a handful of years to 2016. I'd won numerous industry awards, including the National Association of REALTORS 30 Under 30 and Realtor of the Year. By then, I had built a real estate sales team and invested in real estate myself—buying and managing my own properties. While I was thinking about residual income, I was also looking for our next challenge.

My team and I often found ourselves gathered around our conference table in a Long & Foster office that we had already outgrown, brainstorming ideas for ways to grapple with the same challenge I first realized at the beginning of my real estate career: How could we ensure we got paid every month without fail, in good markets and in bad ones?

Our research pointed us toward two possible lanes to generate residual income: investment property and property management. We chose the latter, mainly because of its potential to open doors to the former.

Many people choose to invest in real estate to build wealth. I thought property management might be my opportunity to do just that—and to do it even more effectively than I could have otherwise.

With property management, I could get my hands on large portfolios of property that I myself might want to purchase at some point down the line. In the meantime, I'd have the chance to learn firsthand from property owners who had built tremendous wealth through property acquisition. With their insights, I could better evaluate property purchasing opportunities.

I would also learn that building a property management division would offer numerous other rewards—so many more than I had first anticipated. Property management wouldn't just get me in the door to more real estate investment deals; it would provide access to an entirely new niche market, one that was very different from traditional residential sales. Soon, my team and I were connecting with multiple investors and eventually became a broker for investor-to-investor transactions.

We began to see that the ceiling on opportunities spawned by property management was much, much greater than we'd originally thought. By working with landlords and tenants, we vastly broadened our list of potential sales clients.

Equally important, as we planned, hired, and executed strategically to meet our management responsibilities, we discovered new opportunities to "bolt on" ancillary service businesses, such as plumbing, remodeling, and maintenance, that supported our clients' needs—all while creating new "income silos." Like Amazon or Apple, once we brought clients into our ecosystem, we were able to sell them multiple products and services—and offer them an unparalleled customer service experience. As a result, they kept coming back.

Let's take a closer look at some of the reasons my team and I chose right in deciding to build a property management business—and why you should consider doing the same.

Property Management Can Better Meet the Needs of Existing Clients

While we understood that most of our sales clients needed insurance, mortgages, and title insurance, we also knew that some of them required the services of a good property manager. Meanwhile, we already had a trusting business relationship with our customers. *Why, we wondered, should we send them out the door to look for a good property manager when we ourselves could fulfill their needs?*

When we began building our property management business, we looked to companies leading the way in creating fast, easy solutions for customers—such as Amazon, Apple, and Uber.

With their business models in mind, we set out to create ancillary businesses that would conveniently satisfy all the various needs of our real estate customers—thus taking a one-stop-shop approach to real estate.

Our clients confirmed that we had the right strategy, telling us that our wraparound approach was proving invaluable.

A Property Management Account Can Generate Income for Several Years— and Create a Powerful Sales Pipeline

According to the National Association of REALTORS, although a former sales client may refer new business to you, they probably won't buy or sell with you again for about five years. In contrast, a property management account will likely produce steady income, including rent percentages and leasing fees, for several years.

As a bonus, your managed properties will also generate new sales. Some of your tenants will inevitably become buyers. When they see how capable you are at handling their needs as tenants, they'll be ready and willing to engage your services when it's time to purchase a home.

And if something comes up and they need property management services, they know who to call. For example, a number of times we have sold a tenant a home of their own, only to hear a few months later that they are relocating due to a new job or family obligation.

Rather than sell the property they just purchased, they entrust us with its management, enabling them to make a move while still collecting rental income (and resting assured that their home is in good hands). Often, we manage their properties for years, until they decide to sell or move back.

Landlords provide another pipeline opportunity. Traditional landlords typically own multiple properties, and when you service one well, they are likely to bring you on to manage the others—especially since many of them have had negative experiences with other property management businesses in the past. In addition, the landlords you work with may eventually sell their properties or buy new ones to add to their portfolio—providing you with another chance to make a sale.

This dynamic has been particularly effective for our sales business, as the United States is currently facing a housing shortage. While other real estate businesses may be struggling to find inventory at the moment, we're not. Why? The landlords we work with realize the value of our partnership and, thus, trust us to sell their properties when the time comes.

We're also holding on to our property management accounts and then some, as investors are buying more buildings due to today's rock-bottom interest rates. It's further evidence that we've built a broad-reaching, tech company–like ecosystem that enables us to engage buyers in multiple ways, year after year.

How much will your sales grow as a result of your management activities? Our portfolio of twelve hundred properties generates an average of $10 million to $12 million in volume each year. This number has begun increasing, accounting for more than one hundred sales—and we see it growing to more than $20 million in volume down the line.

In fact, our largest transaction ever was for a property that we managed—an apartment complex worth $7 million. (And, by the way, I was the buyer!)

Property Management Produces Steady Income in *All* Markets

Why is property management income so reliable? Whether the economy is strong or weak, people still need a place to live—and those places must be maintained. Thus, unlike sales earnings, management income does not fluctuate significantly.

Once you have built up a number of accounts, you should start to see stability in good markets and in bad ones. While you may experience explosive growth during certain periods, over time things typically level off and transition into steady, predictable growth.

Because landlords tend to hold on to properties for a long period of time, most clients are long term, bolstering that predictability. Even in the worst of market conditions, it's unlikely that 50 percent of your owners would sell their properties. And if they do sell, they may buy new properties to replace what they've given up. As of this writing, for example, we're seeing lots of landlords purchase multifamily homes because interest rates are so low.

During the recession of 2008 and 2009—the worst my team and I have ever seen—our management business was still solid. This was prior to our real growth, when we were still a small company—but solid nonetheless. Many people flocked to rentals due to foreclosures, or because they were scared to purchase a house amid so much uncertainty. Likewise, as I write this a year into the COVID-19 shutdown, our management proceeds have remained strong, since the vast majority of our tenants continued to pay their rent, and people are purchasing homes or remaining in their current residences to stay safe.

Property Management Presents Other Opportunities for Expansion

But the buck doesn't stop at stability. Property management offers the opportunity for expansion into a multitude of areas. Property managers rely on the services of plumbers, electricians, groundskeepers, HVAC technicians, carpenters, and others to keep facilities running smoothly. As I mentioned, once your portfolio of properties begins to grow, you may find it wise to form profitable partnerships with such service providers—or to create your own service companies to meet those needs, thus establishing additional silos of income.

Later on, we'll talk about the ins and outs of building out ancillary businesses, but for now it's worth noting that multiple offerings like these help you create that tech-like ecosystem that provides value to your operation and to your clients.

Over Time, Property Management Income Far Exceeds Per-Unit Sales

While a typical sales commission might be $10,000, long-term income from a single managed property may total two or three times that amount, depending upon how long you manage the property—and on the market you're in.

For example, in New York City, where the average home sale price is $725,000 as of February 2021, that may not be the case.[1] But often, you can easily out-earn a one-time commission with a property management account, as multiple leasing commissions (which you receive each time the home is rented), residual monthly income, and some of the ancillary services we'll discuss later on rack up over the years.

Add to that one or more home sales to tenants and/or to the landlord, and you could be looking at six or seven different transactions generated by the same unit, compared to just one. I've seen the following situation unfold multiple times: A landlord approaches us to manage her property, and a tenant moves in. When the tenant's lease is up, we sell the tenant a house.

Meanwhile, the landlord has us replace the HVAC system and put in new floors. Eventually, she purchases additional properties

---

1   Marco Santarelli, "New York Real Estate Market: Prices | Trends | Forecast 2021," Norada Real Estate Investments, February 23, 2012, https://www.noradarealestate. com/blog/new-york-real-estate-market/#:~:text=Data%20by%20Redfin.com%20 shows,down%209.36%25%20since%20last%20year.

through us as well. She then recommends us to her family, friends, and other landlords. And when she's ready to sell the original property, she asks us to help with the sale as well.

You can see how one income-generating event turns into many.

Once You Learn the Ropes, You'll Be Better Equipped to Invest Yourself

Owning investment property is a great way to build wealth. By leveraging the knowledge we've acquired from managing property, several of my teammates and I have successfully added rental properties to our personal portfolios. We'll discuss this in greater detail in another chapter, but I'll share an example from my own portfolio that's worth considering until then.

Owning an apartment complex had always been on my bucket list, but I never could have anticipated how quickly I'd be able to realize it.

> *Owning investment property is a great way to build wealth.*

My team and I took over a 120-unit complex that had been very poorly managed. In righting the wrongs introduced by the previous management company, I learned how to run every aspect of a large complex effectively, from instituting a budget and making necessary repairs to marketing.

Shortly after we turned it around, the landlord told me that he was so happy with our work that if I ever wanted to buy it, he'd sell it to me.

One day, just about three years after we began managing the property, he called and asked me to buy it.

With deals as big as this one, there's often a very short window to make a decision. This situation was no different. But at that point, I knew virtually everything there was to know about the project, including the expenses. I had had three years to get comfortable with it. What could have been a complex and difficult decision, made more challenging due to time pressure, was essentially a no-brainer.

If I hadn't managed the complex myself, however, I never would have felt comfortable pulling the trigger on the purchase.

Since then, I have been able to do the same for other properties—choosing to sign on the dotted line because I knew exactly what I was getting myself into. In each case, I didn't have to rely on others' data; I had my own, all of which had been gathered in real time.

A Business with Predictable Residual Income Is a More Salable Asset

Since so many factors can affect your sales business, your company will be more attractive to potential purchasers (should you one day decide to sell) if you can support your valuation by pointing to a strong stream of predictable residual income.

I've experienced this firsthand. A couple years ago, someone expressed interest in purchasing my business. I was quite surprised by the amount of value given to the property management arm due to the amount of residual income it generated. Ultimately, it was less about profitability than the fixed amount of funds we generated each month.

Those with a Strong Foundation in Sales Typically Grow Quite Quickly

If you are already successful in sales, and if you build your management company properly, you can expect to acquire several hundred properties in one to two years. Why? You have a huge book of business on which to draw already. You have clients, you have investors, and you're known in the community. That's way more than half the battle.

To generate interest and attract clients, all you have to do is tap into your existing sphere of influence. That's what my team and I did, marketing to those in our database. In fact, many of the massive leaps we experienced in terms of growth were due to relationships I had already built.

We were able to secure three to four hundred units in just eighteen months, due in large part to those existing relationships. And by carrying over much of what we'd learned from sales, we were able to grow from zero to twelve hundred managed units in just four-and-a-half years.

Moreover, as our property management market share grew, our entire company benefited from increased visibility, which in turn bolstered our sales numbers.

Being Better Than the Competition Gives You a Major Leg Up

Finally, I'll quietly mention another factor that helped us grow our management business: others' shortcomings.

Quite simply, many property managers simply do not do a good job as compared to (in my opinion) a good operator for a sales team.

If they're just focused on property management, they don't have the economies of scale that your sales team already has, and a lot of times they are filling a void because there are no competitors. I have found that in most markets, most management companies are small mom-and-pops with standalone businesses, or huge institutional organizations that only focus on managing their own product. They also lack the operational infrastructure and marketing acumen of a good sales team. As a result, they fail to coordinate effectively with landlords and tenants, are brusque during interactions or hard to get ahold of, charge high rates for small or poorly done services, mismanage budgets, and more. Meanwhile, landlords and tenants expect and deserve professional service. If they don't receive it, they'll move on to greener pastures. And when they do find them, they'll stick around—and tell their peers.

If you already run a successful sales team, you come in with a serious competitive advantage. That means with a little hard work, foresight, and Miracle-Gro, you can secure their business for years to come.

Of course, it's not all grassy knolls, sunshine, and rainbows. In the next chapter, we'll talk about some of the common challenges you may encounter when establishing your property management business—including some hilarious and horrifying stories from my own files—and touch on what to do about them.

Key Insights

- Property management offers you an opportunity to establish profitable, years-long relationships with new or existing clients who seek easy solutions to their management needs.

- A property management business creates a built-in pipeline of sales clients. Many tenants will eventually purchase homes. Similarly, landlords may in time buy additional properties or sell ones that they no longer want. And when they do, you'll be top of mind. On average, we have seen a more than $10 million increase in volume and around one hundred units a year, and the numbers are only going up.

- Income from property management remains steady in both strong and weak real estate markets.

- You can create new silos of income by establishing your own service companies: plumbing, HVAC, remodeling, electrical, and more.

- Over time, profits from one managed property will far exceed what you might expect to earn in commission from a single sales transaction.

- Learning the ropes of property management will prepare you and your team members to confidently purchase investment properties for your personal portfolios.

- Your business will become a more salable asset if your income includes steady, predictable cash generated by a property management division.

- Real estate pros with a strong foundation in sales can expect to ramp up their management companies quickly, acquiring hundreds of properties within one or two years.

- There is a huge niche market in property management that is underserviced—and most markets lack serious competitors. That means you have an entire blue ocean in which to scale. If you treat your clients well, they will value your services and tell their friends.

CHAPTER 2

THE CHALLENGES OF BUILDING A PROPERTY MANAGEMENT BUSINESS

While there are plenty of pros to starting a property management business, as with any venture, there are cons too—and it's crucial to consider the challenges ahead before you commit.

Property management is not like sales. Rather, it is a demanding, 24/7 business that is adversarial in nature—as tenants and landlords often find themselves facing off. And both parties definitely present unique challenges. Take the tenant who frequently called our office insisting that there was a bat in her apartment. Though she swore otherwise, every time my team came to check things out, nothing was there. Months later, we realized the real reason for her calls: she just wanted to move to a first-floor unit, and she thought the threat of a spooky flying rodent would be her ticket into one.

Complaining about issues, real or imagined, incessantly isn't unusual. Our team fielded calls from one tenant who was an actual rocket scientist and insisted the place's HVAC wasn't as efficient as it could be—going so far as to explain the issue by drawing the house and its various systems to scale, including every piece of his furniture, before hand delivering it to our office.

You'll soon find that tenants also find ways to break the seemingly unbreakable. One man called us to share that he had heard a ghost in his rental. But that wasn't all. He had crawled into the pull-down attic to find it, only to fall through the ceiling—which now required a significant repair. Based on his logic, which turned out to be as nebulous as the ghost itself, he wasn't liable for the damage.

Of course, many of the situations we encounter are more run-of-the-mill, but just as frustrating to manage. Often, a simple maintenance issue—like a broken lightbulb—leads tenants to believe they're not responsible for the rent for the duration it's out, for example. Requests to make a year's worth of rent payments in cash up front, sort out romantic relationship drama by adding or subtracting names from a lease, and to return security deposits even though tenants have destroyed their temporary homes are all par for the course.

Just ask the parents who were cosigners on their college student's lease. When their kid forgot to leave the heat on in the house over winter break and all the pipes burst, they were sure they weren't responsible. Unfortunately for them, neither the landlord nor the court in which he sued them agreed. But it was our team who had to handle the brunt of both parties' frustration.

Don't get me wrong: landlords can create their fair share of issues too. Some property owners demand to keep those precious security deposits unfairly despite our warnings, only to find themselves in court on the wrong end of a lawsuit. They show up to their properties unannounced to collect funds when someone doesn't pay—a major no-no. And sometimes they try to respond to a service call themselves and fix a problem to avoid a fee—another move that just isn't okay. (These are the kinds of owners, as my team and I have learned over time and elaborate on in later chapters, that you don't want to keep in your portfolio.)

Both landlords' and tenants' motives are understandable: property owners want to get the best ROI they can, and that can mean getting the work they need done for the best deal possible. That desire is often at odds with tenants' primary goal: to get the best rental and service for their money. Meanwhile, by the very nature of the role, the property manager is caught in the middle of that mess—though it's technically your job to represent and protect the owner, even when you can see the tenant's side of things.

That's further compounded by the fact that property managers have skin in the game when it comes to hiring contractors to do any necessary work. You, too, must

> *Prepare to put out fires, occasionally literal ones, all day and deep into the night.*

look out for your bottom line, getting the best price for the work that must be done. And when contractors run into problems along the way, guess who they call? That's right, they, too, have you on speed dial. Put all those voices—tenants, landlords, and contractors—on a 24/7 loop, and you've got a glimpse into what life looks like when you're running a busy property management business. Prepare to put out fires, occasionally literal ones, all day and deep into the night.

The characteristics of the job make burnout an all-too-common reality for staff. It's an often thankless job that requires thick skin and the moxie to push back against whoever's in the wrong. Nevertheless, it is a business that handsomely rewards those who properly and methodically prepare to meet its unique challenges.

We'll talk about how to do that here, including the struggles that can arise on the way to establishing a foundation that will support your success today and tomorrow—and how to counter them from the very beginning.

Before you accept your first clients, you will need to structure your business properly, carefully project costs and profitability, build out the required systems and infrastructure, and hire wisely. Let's get into the nuts and bolts of how to do that.

Keep Things Separate

First off, there's something crucial you must do to avoid a challenge with particularly serious consequences: it is critical that you ensure your sales and management businesses are separate from the start.

That means establishing separate corporations, phone lines, bank accounts, and even websites.

Why is this move so important? I've mentioned the adversarial nature of property management. Any of the parties you're working with—tenants, landlords, or vendors—may become disgruntled for reasons for which you may or may not be responsible during your relationship. If they funnel that frustration into a lawsuit against your property management company, the separation between that operation and your sales business will ensure that your sales operation is protected.

With potential liability in mind, the names and branding of your companies should differ entirely too. That offers yet another layer of protection to each of your enterprises, especially since the challenge of property management inevitably results in negative reviews from time to time—which you'll want to keep isolated from your other organizations. Having different identities for your businesses also cuts down on confusion. You won't have to worry about people calling your service line when they're attempting to reach sales, or vice versa. Meanwhile, those with whom you've connected through sales or property management and directed to the other arm of your operation won't question the distinction, since you've made the hand-off yourself. It's a lesson I learned a bit too late, and one I hope you'll take to heart as you set out on your own path.

With a sound structure in place, you can get into the nitty-gritty, working with your CPA and attorney to choose an appropriate legal structure.

You must be mindful that the legal structure you choose will affect your taxes and the overall efficiency of your entire operation, so it's vital to ensure that your legal and financial team has the knowledge to ensure your structure is providing you with the best tax advantages possible and establishing smooth operations from the get-go.

In our case, for example, we have created an additional, stand-alone corporation alongside our sales and property management organizations whose primary purpose is to handle accounts payable—including payroll. This setup makes it easier for us to track expenses and profit across our company. The arrangement also provides legal protection by isolating any potential lawsuits that might result from employee grievances.

Although laws affecting incorporation vary by state, the key advantages of structuring strategically remain relatively static across borders. In the next chapter, we'll get into the ins and outs of some of our structuring decisions and what they meant for us financially, but before that we've got to talk about the hiring choices that can make or break your business.

Make the Right Hires

This may sound like hyperbole, but I assure you it's not: the quality of your first three hires will determine whether your management business succeeds or fails. As such, you have to hire wisely. Don't cut corners, and don't sacrifice quality to save on salaries. Bringing on the wrong person at a slightly lower rate can result in tremendous costs in the long run—both financially and otherwise.

> *The quality of your first three hires will determine whether your management business succeeds or fails.*

This can be a real challenge because, especially at the beginning, it's a race to scale. You can't make good money until you rack up a number of accounts, but when you reach that goal—and often before then—you need a staff to manage them.

I was fortunate enough to be able to invest money from my successful sales business into building a property management business with the peace of mind that I wouldn't need a return right away. But know that you will likely lose money before you hit your first benchmark, as you'll need great hires to help you build up your business—and those hires cost money. **One of the most important lessons I've learned in business is that you can't hire for where you are; you've got to hire for where you're going.**

I took that perspective to heart when developing our property management arm. There were times when I knew that the business may not have been able to afford an employee right then, but if I thought I could acquire the accounts to cover it in the near future, it was worth it to me to take the risk. Why? Having enough people on board not only ensures you can cover all your bases when it comes to tasks, but it also prevents you and your colleagues from burning out. That became my aim: to bring on someone new *before* others on my team felt the heat of handling too many accounts, not after.

What positions do you need to fill first and foremost? A business-development person to handle leasing, a maintenance coordinator, and a person to handle your accounting. Like the three legs of a stool, each position will prove essential to your operation. Salaries vary depending on your market. While the going rate for a maintenance coordinator may be $50,000 in Maryland, you may find yourself paying $80,000 for the same skill set in California. While every market is different—and, as such, salaries differ as well—you should expect to spend $100,000 to $150,000 in salaries and infrastructure before you break even.

Do your research to determine an appropriate range for your neck of the woods. My philosophy is that it's important to pay your people well from the outset and to keep doing so once your business is established. The nature of this industry makes it tough to attract and keep good people, and that means it's worth your while to compensate them as best you can and to reward ongoing performance. If you hire someone at a lower rate, chances are you're going to pay for it in more ways than one.

Also be aware that the people you bring on board will need to be thick-skinned. Some might describe these positions as somewhat "thankless," as property management employees can expect to be yelled at frequently by upset landlords and tenants. What personality type succeeds in such a job? Someone whose nature differs somewhat from that of the typical salesperson—someone with a little grit, as it will be an invaluable trait in any hire you make. Any time I've deviated from using grit as a primary hiring criterion, it has backfired.

How do you know when a potential hire has grit? I highly recommend reading *Grit: The Power of Passion and Perseverance* by Angela Duckworth, which explores the trait—and the science behind its value—in depth. Those who don't have it just won't last.

We'll cover this in greater detail shortly, but for now, one final word to the wise on hiring: don't overlook red flags in favor of filling a spot, saving some cash, or helping someone in your network. I promise, you'll regret it.

Build Out Your Projections

Once you've thought about structure, both in terms of the framework you'll develop and who you'll bring on to run things on a daily basis, it's time to consider your finances. Before you even begin the process of building your property management business, you must carefully estimate what you will spend on salaries and infrastructure. After all, you want to recoup your investment—and then some. If you make the wrong financial decisions up front, failing to take into account all the start-up costs, you could find yourself in a veritable money pit ... minus the charm of upstate New York and Tom Hanks.

So crunch the numbers, adding up the probable yearly costs for phones, your website, software, and marketing (including social media advertising). Then, plug in the likely salaries of your first three hires.

Once you have projected these expenses, you can divide your total by the annual income that you expect to receive from your average property account. The quotient will indicate the number of accounts you will need to acquire in order to break even on your costs.

For example, let's imagine that my CFO and I have projected $125,000 in costs for the next year.

With that number in mind, we'll look at income. Our management company's typical commission fee is $100 per month per property—10 percent of our average rent charge of $1,000. We also collect an initial leasing fee equal to the first month's rent for each unit.

Thus, one property would generate $2,100 in its first year: a $1,000 leasing fee + $100 x 11 months.

Now, we divide that annual income per unit into our projected yearly expenses of $125,000. The quotient, 59.5, represents the number of properties we will need to manage in order to break even.

With that said, it's time for a harsh reality: you should not expect to arrive at your break-even point for about a year.

As such, I encourage you to study your numbers thoroughly and dispassionately. Will your present savings and other income support such a venture? If not, you likely have some more planning to do before you can launch.

The Cost of Growth

Although doing so may seem premature, you should also estimate the costs of scaling your business once you reach profitability. Ask yourself, *How many accounts will I aim for? Five hundred? One thousand?*

Keep in mind that expenses will grow alongside your business, as you'll need more people and resources to handle the additional load. For example, when it comes to labor costs—based on my experience—your first three hires should be able to manage three hundred to four hundred accounts. As you exceed those numbers, you will need to add one additional employee for every one hundred new accounts you bring on. As such, there's another question to ask yourself as you think through the potential challenges and opportunities a property management business can pose: *As I grow, how many additional accounts will I need to cover my increased costs?* You can see that it quickly becomes a balancing act of bringing on enough accounts and enough resources to keep things running smoothly as you make progress toward your expansion goals.

What's the best way to plan for future growth? Start with the end in mind. I always recommend that you focus on your end goals and then work backward, or "reverse engineer," to determine what steps will enable you to achieve those goals. Be diligent. Watch out for those challenges from the beginning, so you can anticipate them. Then, plan thoughtfully, thoroughly, and accordingly.

Note, too, that you must sweat the small stuff alongside the bigger issues.

Pay Attention to P&L in Real Time

Property management is a high-volume, low-margin business. It can be extremely lucrative on a large scale. We can look at a single property management account to see just how much it can produce over time.

Suppose you manage a rental for three years. Over that period, your monthly fees might total $5,000. Add a leasing commission of $1,500, and your revenue increases to $6,500.

Then, perhaps, the landlord buys one or two properties from you, and you make, say, $8,000 in commission per property. Now you've generated $15,000 or $16,000 from that single property account.

Next, the tenant buys a house through you. If it happens to be the house owned by the landlord (and we've seen this happen often), you double-end a commission from that property. Sound good so far?

If you also have ancillary companies—title insurance, mortgage, plumbing, remodeling, etc.—you might spin off another $5,000 during the life of the account. So that single account, which would initially produce a small amount of money, could potentially generate $25,000 or $30,000. Certainly, all accounts won't do so, but the majority of them will create a substantial amount of income—and that's what's so special about property management.

Now at this point you may wonder, "What is the life span of a typical management account?" There are generally two types of accounts: the accidental landlord who bought when the market may have been hot and had to relocate, or someone who has relocated for whatever reason and decided not to sell. Generally, we see these owners hold for a few years, or whenever a market cycle turns in their favor. The long-term investor will usually hold on to their property for seven to ten years at a minimum, if not more, as their outlook is way longer and they are not as worried about market cycles. Note that this does change if the market gets really hot. Owners with multifamily properties—duplexes, apartments, etc.—tend to hold for a very long time, so you'll see variations in your portfolio.

From a leasing side, you can expect about 25 percent of your account portfolio to turn over each year—and naturally you will have some attrition of accounts from owners selling, tenants buying the properties, and what have you. Keep this percentage in mind—as well as your attrition rate—as you project future costs and revenues to make sure you are always bringing in more accounts than you are losing to be profitable.

Even with large-scale and long-term potential, if you are not in the weeds studying your profit-and-loss (P&L) statement every day, you could potentially lose money. And with small accounts like the ones you'll typically have at the beginning of your journey, every dollar counts. We used to operate as many property management businesses do, reconciling our accounts with a CPA or bookkeeper every quarter. But we found that that led to mistakes along the way, many of which we didn't recognize until sometime down the line—due in large part to the fact that we weren't on top of our P&L statements in the way we should have been.

So if you haven't already done so, adopt an accounting system that will allow you to review your P&L in real time, not just quarterly. And—this is imperative—make that change *before* you launch your property management business. You also have to make sure your systems are in tip-top shape.

Craft Effective Systems

One of the key challenges you'll face will be creating a system that efficiently processes and dispenses the rent money that comes through your business. Handle this chore well, and you will please your landlords and tenants—and easily outshine your less-efficient competition.

To do that, my team uses a software package called AppFolio, which helps us distribute rent payments to landlords (via ACH) in the first seven to ten days of the month. Then, on each subsequent Friday of the month, we distribute any new money that has come in—including late payments. That means those who own multiple properties may receive payment as their tenants pay rent on the first Friday of the month and every subsequent Friday as the money rolls in. Because we're paying shortly after we receive the money, rather than waiting until everything comes through to cut a check, landlords are in a better position financially.

Most property management companies, I'll note, don't do this. Rather, they don't reconcile until the middle or end of the month—a challenge for landlords who have their own mortgages and other bills to pay. That makes paying early and often an absolute game changer in terms of differentiation. We collect payments quickly and send them off as soon as possible, ensuring effective cashflow for property owners and thus preventing them from having to front the money from rent payments before those funds have hit their bank accounts.

Our system of dispersing funds on subsequent Fridays works well for us too. It allows our accounting person to stay organized, while freeing her from the burden of processing payments every single day. Thus, she has the time and space to take on new tasks and develop professionally. And it's yet another way to cut down on some of the challenges that pop up by being proactive.

What other steps can you take to reduce challenges and promote operational efficiency? First, choose a software program that provides 24/7 online account visibility to your tenants and landlords. Second—and I wholeheartedly recommend this if it is appropriate for your market: advise your tenants that you will only accept online payments. Such a policy will save you a lot of time.

Of course, you must institute systems for aspects of your business other than financials—many of which can also be managed through the software programs you choose.

For instance, regardless of the software system you employ, make sure to route all your maintenance requests through that system. It is imperative, too, that you select a system that has an inbound call system to take the maintenance calls. Or you can outsource this task and have it run through the system early on in your career. The alternative—having your employees answer maintenance-related phone calls all day—is a time-guzzler and simply not acceptable nor scalable, especially when you consider that the software will handle the requests so efficiently.

In fact, even if a requestor—say, a friendly landlord whom you know well—phones you personally, you should say, "You have to call the maintenance line." Make sure the request goes into your system. I can't stress enough how much time and effort these programs will save you.

A good program will link a tenant's or landlord's request to the proper account, document all communication, and follow the work order through the entire repair process.

Price Your Services Right

Another challenge comes in the form of pricing. To stay competitive and avoid unforeseen issues, you've got to get it right. As a rule of thumb, I recommend that you charge a leasing commission equal to a full month's rent and, thereafter, a management fee equal to 10 percent of the monthly rent for a property.

Depending on your market, you may be able to charge as much as 12 or 13 percent, but don't go below 10 percent, even if you have competitors who are willing to do so.

Why? You certainly never want to be the cheapest management company out there—unless you want to join a self-destructive race to the bottom. (There is one exception here: If a multiunit owner offers you fifty or sixty accounts, you may wish to extend a discount, but even under these circumstances, be careful. Understand your costs, and don't place yourself in a position to lose money.)

There is another reason why you should generally not discount your fees. If you do so, you will attract stingy landlords who will bicker with you each time you ask them to authorize even a small $100 repair. We've worked with such people, and they have fought with us over everything. As a result of this misstep, we suffered additional liability exposure with our tenants, and the time we wasted was not worth the money that the accounts were earning.

Now you may ask, "Are there other ways to weed out potential skinflints?" The answer is yes. Note the landlord's behavior after you initially inspect the property. If the person is unwilling to make necessary repairs before you even rent the property, they would probably maintain that approach after any tenants have arrived.

Here's a second strategy to avoid doing business with cheapskates. If it's customary in your market, you might also consider charging an administrative fee to set up the new account. Hearing about that $100 fee, in addition to your other charges, will cause a cheap landlord to head for the hills and inquire elsewhere—and save you a lot of frustration down the line.

Stay on Track

It's not enough to start out on the right path; you must also stay on track with ongoing attention and management. Salespeople have a reputation for not always being the best organized. You just don't have that option with property management if you want to be successful.

Organization, diligence, and planning are musts to thrive in this business. Fortunately, with the strategies we've outlined here, you should be well positioned to build and run a solid operation: enlist your CPA and attorney to design your structure, plan meticulously, hire carefully, build your infrastructure, and work efficiently. Your reward will be a lucrative and scalable enterprise.

Now that we've laid out some of the challenges that can arise— and how to counter them—let's dig a bit deeper into the financial side of things and the benefits a knowledgeable resource can provide.

Key Insights

- Unlike sales, property management is a demanding, 24/7 business that is adversarial in nature, as tensions frequently arise between landlords and tenants. First and foremost, ask yourself if you're up for the challenge.

- It is critical that you separate your property management business from your sales business. With the help of your attorney and your CPA, you should also structure your businesses to maximize efficiency and limit liability.

- Hire carefully. Your first three employees (accounting person, maintenance coordinator, and business developer) will make or break your property management business.

- Before beginning the process of building your property management company, carefully estimate costs, revenue, and the number of accounts you will need in order to break even. Expect to spend $100,000 to $150,000 in salaries and other costs before you reach profitability.

- Plan for growth. Determine the number of accounts that you would like to have, then reverse engineer to identify the steps you'll need to take to reach your goals.

- To ensure long-term success, stay on top of your P&L every day.

- Establish effective systems for everything from payment processing to maintenance requests to avoid labor-intensive processes and other issues.

- Charge fees appropriate for your market, and do not attempt to undercut your competition. Discounting your rates will only come to bite you in the end, attracting cheap, uncooperative landlords.

CHAPTER 3

TAKING A SAVVY FINANCIAL APPROACH

Real estate has long been a tool harnessed by wealthy people to increase their assets and net worth. But you don't need a host of zeros to your name to access its benefits. By now you know that to do so, it's critical to set out with a strong financial plan, as the structures and budgeting you do up front will set you up for success. But as you may have guessed, savvy financial management doesn't end there.

Real estate provides numerous opportunities that you can harness over time, opportunities that will protect you and your business, save you money on taxes, and help you build more wealth—which is likely why you got into the industry in the first place. But you can only take advantage of all the benefits available to you, like depreciation and cost segregation, if you know they're there—and how to use them. That's yet another reason why you need a strong and knowledgeable team—which may be as lean as a CPA and attorney to start—to help guide you in the right direction today and tomorrow.

With that in mind, let's explore some money-saving and profit-earning strategies a financial expert can help you employ to achieve your maximum potential. Note that many of the insights in this chapter are courtesy of Sara Lavdas, our company's chief financial officer. Sara has been a CPA for more than fifteen years and has provided us with invaluable advice on structuring our business, creating LLCs, investing in rental property, and saving on taxes. In fact, the exceptional insight and support she provided as our accountant led us to bring her on as CFO.

So without further ado, let's talk about what you can do with effective financial strategies—including the right advice—starting with how we structured our property management business.

Structuring Your Business

First and foremost, as I mentioned in the previous chapter, we started out with separation. Our company owns at least a hundred residential

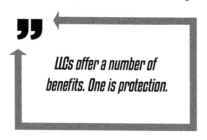

LLCs offer a number of benefits. One is protection.

rental properties, and all of them are inside limited liability companies (or LLCs), which are legal entities. LLCs offer a number of benefits. One is protection. When you start a business inside an LLC, you're not personally on the hook for any business liabilities. Thus, I was able to shield myself from liability that would attach to me personally if I owned the properties in my own name. It's possible to put several properties—perhaps ones that are located near one another—into one LLC, and to then place others into additional LLCs. That way, if something bad happens in one particular property, that property won't damage, or align itself with, all your others, another beneficial element of this option. LLCs also make record-keeping pretty simple, as opposed to the rules and regulations for corporations, which are much stricter. They also provide the opportunity for tax savings. Sara took all these factors into account when advising on how to set things up.

What does our structure look like at large?

We have one umbrella company that owns most of our primary operations, but inside that company, we set up three different segments. One segment is property management, and it has its own limited liability company. A second segment is sales, and it also has its own LLC. And then we have a third segment—also an LLC—that carries all our accounts payable, including our vendors and our payroll.

Why do we have a separate entity to handle payroll and vendors? There are a couple of reasons, the first being tax related. There are a lot of tax rules associated with how you pay people. If you have one main entity that covers payroll, you can allocate that expense to your other entities and see more easily—from an investment standpoint—how profitable you are. We also discussed an LLC's ability to provide legal protection, and that benefit applies here too. Say an employee were to bring a malpractice suit against you. If you had a single LLC that just handled payroll, that action would be isolated to that LLC alone, shielding the rest of your operation from financial liability. And, I repeat, there is a very good chance that you will be sued by someone at some point or another, so it's prudent to prioritize legal protection.

A sound structure is just one piece of the financial puzzle. You can also reap tremendous individual benefits when it comes to handling investment properties.

Making Smart Investments

I'm a huge proponent of owning real estate—particularly for those who work in the industry. It's a great way to build wealth and long-term residual income. Surprisingly though, a lot of people in our business don't know about all the tax and investment benefits that come with buying and renting residential property, especially if the buyer's principal business is real estate.

One of the primary reasons owning and renting real estate is profitable is due to *depreciation*. We all know that, historically, real estate values increase over time—inching up most years. Well, the IRS doesn't really consider that reality. In fact, it allows you to take a portion of the amount you paid to purchase a property and deduct that fractional amount on your tax return *each year*. It's a real deduction, but it's a fake expense, because you're not actually laying out any new cash year after year, and in fact the asset is most likely appreciating.

Better yet, if your deduction is large enough, there's a chance that you could have positive cash flow in reality, but on paper and to the IRS, you could be losing money. Now, there aren't many businesses where you can make a profit but actually show a loss. Making a smart investment with a good depreciation strategy is the best way to go when it comes to real estate.

Here's an example: This year, you decide to buy a $200,000 property—residential real estate—as an investment. You'll receive a settlement sheet that reflects the purchase price. It's important to note that you can only depreciate the building, not the land. If you don't want to pay for a land appraisal, you can head to your state's tax assessment website where you can determine how much of the total cost applies to the building you purchased and how much applies to the land.

Let's say 20 percent of the tax assessment applies to the land. Twenty percent of your $200,000 purchase price would be $40,000. The remainder, $160,000 of value, would be allocated to the building. With residential rental property, you get to write off an equal share of that amount for 27.5 years ($160,000 ÷ 27.5 would produce a yearly deduction of $5,818).

So about 3.5 percent gets deducted the first year you place the house into rental service, and 3.5 percent comes off again and again every year after that—even though, in reality, the property is probably increasing in value. That's where the savings come in.

I recently learned about another benefit—something I'd never learned about over the course of my career. Our company purchased an apartment complex and received a substantial write-down on our taxes, thanks to Sara's guidance. The big-time benefit we got comes from a process called *cost segregation.*

To understand cost segregation, it's important to note that the government likely views investing in real estate as a boon for the economy, as the IRS treats real estate investors very favorably. One benefit investors can capitalize on is called bonus depreciation. Initially, it allowed you to take a 50 percent deduction on the purchase of new personal property in the year you put the property into service and was mostly used for equipment and vehicles. Recently, though, the IRS has allowed for a 100 percent write-off and expanded this to used property and some real property types. Now, you can't take 100 percent of a full building, but you can break the building down into smaller pieces. To do that, you can use cost segregation.

A cost segregation expert can do a formal report by inspecting the property and identifying the value of some of the building's components for you. They do that by going into the building you purchased and dictating how much various elements of it are worth, from the light fixtures to the appliances.

With my apartment building—a very large purchase—numerous items had been identified and valued, including the window blinds and fire extinguishers. Ultimately, we accounted for so many items that their value totaled about 25 percent of the entire purchase. Importantly, those items had depreciation periods of fifteen years or less and were eligible for a 100 percent write-off in the first year we owned the building! That led to significant savings, thanks to a write-off of over $1 million. When you consider that amount multiplied by your ordinary income tax rate—which could be 37 percent or more—you're saving a lot of money!

Now, that's somewhat of an extreme example—it was a $7 million apartment complex after all, but even on a smaller scale, it could make a major difference. And considering we paid less than $10,000 for the valuation, the knowledge, insight, and investment paid off significantly.

You can go through the same process with a single-family home, getting a valuation on appliances and more and writing off their cost during the first year of ownership. A CPA can handle smaller projects like those (and their insight will likely be worth it; we wouldn't have even known about the opportunity without Sara's expertise). If you yourself have experience fixing up houses and pricing out such items, you may even be able to manage it yourself. And if you have just a handful of single-family properties, you could hire one expert to conduct a valuation on all of them. There are even internet-based software products that can help you do the report rather inexpensively. Be aware, though, that the IRS will ask for evidence of the values of the components—so it pays to have a physical report.

If you're a real estate professional, the IRS has sweetened the pot even more, as you're eligible for additional tax savings. For example, let's say a landlord has a paper loss on a rental property due to depreciation. If the landlord is a real estate professional, they can deduct all that loss against other sources of income, or even carry the loss forward for several years. The nonpro, however, may be limited in what they can write off.

In other words, a real estate professional who owns rental properties could take a paper loss generated by depreciation even if the properties actually had positive cash flow. And then the person could take that loss and subtract it from, say, their real estate commission income, and then ultimately pay less in taxes. If you're in a higher tax bracket, the savings can be substantial.

The key is to be a real estate professional and to own actual properties, rather than, say, stock in companies that invest in properties. You'll not only get the benefit of wealth building that rental properties provide but also that of a major write-off against your ordinary income.

How do you qualify as a real estate pro in the IRS's eyes? You must spend at least 750 hours per year engaged in real estate–related activities, and more than 50 percent of what you do in any year to earn income must be related to real estate. However, the IRS defines "real estate activities" fairly broadly. You could be building or selling houses, or simply involved in architecture, for instance.

Finding (Financial) Power in Knowledge

Of course, depreciation isn't the only upside of buying residential rentals. Similarly, though, you have to be strategic if you want to harness the opportunities these properties pose. As such, there are a few things you should know when you sign on the dotted line to acquire these properties.

For one thing, how and when you place a building into service can be pretty important when it comes to your tax liability. For example, if you need to paint your property, you should paint it *after* you get a certificate of occupancy. If you paint after you get the certificate, you can write off the painting cost in that year. If you paint *before* you get the certificate, you have to capitalize (meaning "write off") the cost over a period of several years. It may seem insignificant, but those small costs add up.

You can—and should—also make two elections on your tax forms that will make a big difference in the size of your tax bill: *de minimis safe harbor* and *safe harbor for small taxpayers*. If you elect to take advantage of these rules, you can basically write off anything in your rental that costs you less than $2,500. Say you bought a new oven or microwave. You could write that off as soon as you bought it and placed it in service.

What about the rules regarding commercial real estate? The IRS actually treats commercial entities *even more favorably*. If you're aiming to take advantage of depreciation, you can elect what's called Section 179. Though it has some limitations, it's similar to bonus depreciation, allowing you to write off a large amount during the first year you place a property in service.

If you have a tenant occupying a commercial rental property and you build the space out for the tenant, you can take advantage of *Qualified Improvement Property*, writing off those improvements in the year in which you place them in service. And those eligible improvements could include a lot of things—basically anything in the interior of the building. If you do wall work, for example, you can deduct that in the first year of service. And, by the way, the Qualified Improvement Property benefit, though only recently signed into law, is retroactive to 2018. It's an important benefit when you consider how costly a tenant build-out can be.

What if you're just starting to consider the potential rental properties could provide for you personally and professionally? Begin by getting your feet wet. Purchase a single-family house or condo to rent out. If you're already in the real estate business, you probably know the going rate for rents and how the market works. Look for a property that will make enough money to cover the mortgage and the essential repairs that you will have to make to fix up the home and maintain it. If you find a good place, there's a chance that just the money you save in taxes will make the investment worth it. And even if someone were to come to you and say, "Well, you can make more money in the stock market," consider that you have to pay full taxes on the money you make there.

Getting the Right Advice

How do you uncover valuable insights like these and strategize accordingly on your own? Some of the concepts we've discussed are complex. To be successful, you must be looking at your expenses on a regular basis and considering how the decisions you make will affect your tax liability today and tomorrow. As such, you can't just go to the pop-up tax shop that appears in your neighborhood at the beginning of each year. Even in the realm of CPAs, real estate knowledge is considered somewhat specialized. That means you need the right accountant with whom to partner, who will be in your corner and call you when changes occur.

For instance, when the CARES Act passed during the coronavirus pandemic, knowledgeable accountants got on the phone and began calling clients to let them know that its passing came with some retroactive tax benefits, and that it was time to amend their returns to get some money back.

Where do you look for a good CPA, someone who will be on top of any changes and available for whatever comes up? Start in your backyard. A local accountant will know the market you're dealing in and may already know you or about you. When you begin the vetting process, ensure they have experience in real estate so they can help you secure the benefits I've mentioned here.

Another key team member to have if you've got the resources? A bookkeeper. As discussed in the previous chapter, in the property management business, you have to know your P&L in real time—you can't look at it quarterly, the way many people in real estate do. A bookkeeper can make sure you're on track. If that's not in your budget at the moment, input the data yourself using a virtual system, but have a CPA or bookkeeper review what you've done, so they can provide insight into what can be capitalized (meaning written off over time) or written off that year. Such advice can save you money as you go.

They can also provide advice on which moves to make, a benefit many companies—especially small ones without an in-house financial team—overlook. As salespeople, we tend to shoot from the hip and move quickly to keep up with the market. Engaging a financial sounding board can help you make the right decisions in every aspect of your business (just think back to the $1 million Sara saved us thanks to her fantastic insights on depreciation!).

By the time we brought on Sara as our CFO, she had already been a key part of our team, providing real-time advice on our books day in and day out. That kind of support is necessary if you're going to build and run multiple companies, and your accounting has to be airtight. You just can't build an effective operation if you and/or your CPA are always playing catch-up.

How did we decide to bring Sara on full time? If you want to scale, you must always think about replacing the tasks you're handling so that you can take on more—and particularly the tasks that aren't your strong suit. I knew where my true strengths lay: in growth, sales, vision, and marketing. Operations and accounting just aren't in my wheelhouse. Further, we had reached a point when we knew we had to bump up our financial support system to keep up with our growth, and hiring a CFO was the next step.

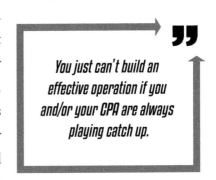

You just can't build an effective operation if you and/or your CPA are always playing catch up.

At that point in our trajectory, we could afford it—a key indicator of whether to go forward with a new hire. We were paying almost as much as a CFO's salary would cost us in accounting expenses anyway, another indicator that it was time to make the switch. Of course, there was some calculated risk involved too. I knew that if I was able to get more financial tasks off my plate, I could do more to grow our companies. (Note: If you're in a similar position but worried about adding a senior leadership salary to your payroll, hiring a lower-level finance person to work in tandem with an outside CPA might be the way to go.)

We knew it would be a challenge to find the right person, so much so that we actually brought on a head-hunting company to find them for us. Since Sara was paying all our bills as our CPA, I sent that one over to her as well.

The day after she received it, she asked if she could come talk to my director of operations and me—something she had never done before. When we sat down that week, she told us that, if we were serious about hiring a CFO, she was interested in the position. To be honest, even if I didn't think I could have afforded her salary request, I would have tried to figure it out, because I knew how talented she was. We had already benefited from her knowledge and experience, and having worked so closely with her over the years, we knew she would be a good cultural fit for our organization. The rest is history, and bringing Sara on board remains one of the best decisions we've ever made.

While Sara's already taken, when looking to outsource a CPA or bring on a full-time staff member, you should consider hiring someone with a similar skill set and perspective. Your financial person should be somewhat risk averse, going after all the details before making a decision; take an analytical approach; and understand the real estate industry so that they can make quick decisions that match the pace of the industry. I'm frequently impressed by Sara's ability to address changes in the tax code or complex problems with our accounts in a very short period of time, explain them in layman's terms, and execute on them almost immediately.

Now, some people will say, "It's expensive to pay for that kind of expertise." And it *is* expensive, but making the wrong decision, spending money you don't necessarily have, or missing a major write-off are all far more costly than getting much-needed help. Plus, the insights of a financial pro will help you make your money back long term—and then some.

Key Insights

- It's critical that you separate your property management business from your sales business.

- You can shield yourself and your various businesses from many legal liabilities by placing the major segments of your company into separate LLCs. You should also place company-owned rental properties into one or more LLCs as well.

- Consider structuring your company so that a separate LLC handles accounts payable (including payroll) for all your divisions. Doing so will provide additional legal protection and make it easier for you to track your profitability.

- Owning residential rental property builds wealth and offers substantial tax benefits.

- If you own rental property, the IRS's generous depreciation policies may allow you to show a loss on your tax forms, even if your property made a profit. Additionally, if you qualify as a "real estate professional," you may be able to deduct the paper loss generated by your rentals against your sales commission income, thus reducing your tax burden.

- Using cost segregation, bonus depreciation, or a Section 179 election may allow you to write off (in your first year) a substantial portion of the cost of an investment property.

- With few exceptions, if you improve the interior of a tenant-occupied commercial property, you may be able to write off those costs in the year in which you placed the improvements into service. This "Qualified Improvement Property" benefit is retroactive to 2018.

- The *de minimis safe harbor* and *safe harbor for small taxpayers* provisions of the tax code will allow you to write off (in the first year) the entire cost of an item purchased for a rental property, provided that the item costs less than $2,500.

- You should be able to review your P&L figures in real time, not just quarterly. Consider using a professional bookkeeper to help if you have the means to do so.

- Hire a certified public accountant who will be in your corner and keep you informed of any beneficial changes in the tax code on a regular basis.

CHAPTER 4

YOUR FIRST THREE HIRES

Now that we've covered the more general elements of building a property management business, let's dig into the details, starting with a crucial component I mentioned in chapter 1: your first three hires—an accounting whiz, a business development associate or leasing director, and a maintenance coordinator. Those three people will be critical to the success of your property management business.

Now, you may not have the luxury of bringing on a staff right off the bat. Oftentimes, the amount of cash you have in the bank dictates whether or not you can make a hire to begin with. But if you can do it, you should.

I should mention that, when my team and I started out in property management, we didn't make those three hires right away.

To begin with, I worked with just one other person and fulfilled that business development role myself. With that said, I believe we would have been able to grow a lot faster had we made those hires earlier on. I was trying to run this new operation like a start-up—on a shoestring budget. Looking back, that was a mistake. If I could go back in time, I would have done what I could to start with the three hires we'll talk about here in place.

Of course, the decision to bring on other employees comes with risk, particularly in the form of capital. Regardless of your financial circumstances, when you hire early in your business's life, it takes time to see a return on that investment. But if you're already running a successful real estate team brokerage and thus have some economies of scale, you can use what you've built in sales to create something new in the property management realm. Those early hires can be a crucial element of your foundation, enabling you to build the kind of business you envision.

With that in mind, we'll cover the tasks associated with each of these positions, the skills and personality traits that you should look for in your candidates, and how to interview to get the information you need and make the right decision.

The Accounting Whiz

An accounting person is vital to your operation, serving as your integrator—the person who will help bring your ideas as the visionary to life. If you only have the budget to make one hire, this is the person to bring on. After all, managing your money correctly from the get-go will be essential to your business's success.

They will oversee all accounting functions of your management business, including the following:

- setting up and monitoring accounts,

- overseeing payments to landlords and contractors,

- recording and disbursing security deposits,

- generating and analyzing reports,

- designing processes, and

- self-managing workflow.

First and foremost, your accounting person must be extremely diligent and very well organized. In fact, that matters more than having a formal accounting background—although they should be "numbers oriented." In fact, our strongest accounting hire had no accounting experience when we brought her on, although she came from the financial world. With her analytical mindset, exceptional organizational skills, and hefty dose of perfectionism, she was an excellent fit for the position.

These skills and tendencies are particularly vital, as they are typically the exact opposite of those a salesperson possesses. While we (salespeople) often shoot from the hip and make decisions based on the information we have in the moment, the right accounting person will want all the data up front before committing to a plan.

Note, too, that they should not only have a knack for numbers but also *enjoy* working with them. Why? Because property management is such a high-volume business, your accounting person will be immersed in figures all day, every day. Those who don't love numbers are much more likely to burn out. And since workloads and stress levels will be high, you also want this "back of the house" employee to have plenty of grit.

The right accounting person is likely to be an introvert as well—yet another difference from a sales personality—preferring to spend their time setting up systems and processes, rather than growing their network. And often, it's those systems and processes that—once they're well established—do most of the work, yet another reason why your accounting hire doesn't have to have a wealth of accounting experience.

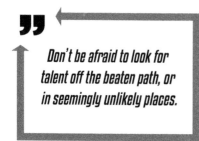

> Don't be afraid to look for talent off the beaten path, or in seemingly unlikely places.

As such, don't be afraid to look for talent off the beaten path, or in seemingly unlikely places. Our first accounting hire was actually my assistant on the sales side and came to me when she heard I was looking to fill the position.

And though it may be tempting to ask your accounting person to multitask and take on a host of different roles—especially when you're just starting out and don't have a lot of cash to burn—you must ensure they're free to focus entirely on financial tasks. You definitely don't want this pivotal person to be fielding phone calls or otherwise dealing with the public; it's just too distracting. Plus, those roles require a different set of skills.

Select this person very carefully; when it comes to money management, they will be the foundational employee upon whose diligence, skill, and expertise you will build your business. Further, be ready to hire others to assist this employee as your business grows and the volume of your accounting chores increases. Otherwise, you'll be opening the door for mistakes.

The Business Development Associate or Leasing Director

Your second hire will be in charge of business development and will also help with leasing, especially in your company's early days. This is your visionary, your big thinker. They will be the person who will go out and get accounts and drive your marketing messaging. In short, they should be a killer salesperson.

If you don't have the money up front, you may find yourself holding this position for a while—especially since your experience running a successful brokerage or real estate team, having a strong pipeline of sales, and being in touch with an established network equip you with the skills and resources for this job.

> I always say that "rich" is measured in dollars, while "wealth" is measured in time.

When you start your management business, you yourself will probably help to bring in new business—especially if you're the rainmaker for your team. Even today, I'm still involved in business development for our property management business, particularly when it comes to securing accounts—due in large part to my network and industry experience. But beware of taking on this role permanently.

I always say that "rich" is measured in dollars, while "wealth" is measured in time. The ultimate mark of success is a business that runs on its own, without your constant guidance—giving you the opportunity to take back your time. Think of it as another investment in which your money works for itself, rather than you continuing to work for the money.

Plus, I couldn't oversee all the companies I do without a high-powered sales team running things for me. If I tried, I'd either burn out myself or end up in an early grave. You should always be thinking, *Where can I replace myself?* And this is one place to do it. That also enables you to focus on your zone of genius, which includes making your business or businesses as much money as possible—not dealing with the day-to-day stuff.

If you already have a real estate sales team, you can also have some members do double duty at the beginning. In the past, we've had members of our marketing team, new agents, and interns fill in on parts of the business development role. But just because you can pinch hit here for a while doesn't mean you can overlook the absolute necessity of creating and filling the business development and leasing position as soon as you can. Keep in mind, too, that while there may be some crossover in terms of roles and responsibilities early on and even once your business is up and running—for example, our marketing director runs marketing for both our real estate sales and property management businesses—leadership roles should always be kept separate.

Look for a strong salesperson who is very good at tracking down leads and following up on them. The best business development associates are extroverts who are able to talk to people and make connections easily. But this can't just be your average seller; they should also have vision to spare—the ability to think globally, not just transactionally. By the same token, they must be able to be in the moment and take care of the customer as needed. And because great salespeople tend to have trouble with the details (they're often too busy thinking big picture), they've got to be great at delegation—making sure that someone else has got the nit-picky stuff covered.

As for hard skills, strong communication abilities, a thorough understanding of marketing, and exceptional copywriting ability are all important.

Ultimately, their goal is to build relationships and rapport with others to secure new projects while building out the sales funnel to get new accounts through all marketing efforts—including social media, direct mail, and more. Staff oversight, hiring, firing, and other HR-related elements will also fall under their purview. In addition, those communication skills will come in handy when a major problem arises, as they will be pulled in to defuse tense situations with landlords and tenants. Think of it as a hybrid CEO-COO position, with a whole host of other responsibilities thrown into the mix, depending on the day.

When we were just starting out, we hired a young man named Shane who was all these things and more. He was and is great with people, very tenacious, and good with marketing. When he started, Shane helped bring in accounts and then helped lease them. Today, he oversees leasing but focuses primarily on acquiring new business. Loaded with grit, he also resolves complaints when problems with landlords or tenants get out of hand. Shane is great at quickly defusing a situation, taking tenant versus landlord disputes down from near-fist-fighting levels to calm conversations that border on "kumbaya."

Over time, you may also discover, as we did, that a role in business development and leasing is a great gateway position for your organization. Why? Hunting down new management accounts serves as excellent training for new hires who eventually want to move into sales. Since the cycle of a lease is so much shorter than a home sale, they have an opportunity to quickly familiarize themselves with sales calls, get used to being told "no," and learn the ins and outs of managing difficult situations—experiences that serve as excellent preparation for the sales side of things. Nowadays, we start all our new salespeople in the leasing department of our property management business. It's a great place for them to learn, and the position allows them the opportunity to earn quick income via the commissions that come through with each lease.

With that said, be sure to fill this role carefully—even if it's just with a pinch hitter from your sales business at first. Why? Because this person carries so much responsibility, putting the wrong person in the position will definitely hurt, setting you back on your path toward growth.

Note, too, that if you determine you don't have the right person in the right seat here, you've got to fire fast. I've made the mistake of keeping someone on too long because I was afraid that if I fired them, the rest of the team would have to pick up the slack. That decision ended up costing me double or triple the work and money in the long run. Why? In each case, we didn't know how bad the situation was until we got rid of them. Making the choice to move on earlier would have saved us countless headaches.

The Maintenance Coordinator

Your third hire will oversee and coordinate all operations involving— you guessed it—maintenance. Beyond handling requests for routine repairs, this employee will manage all activities related to turning over properties: inspections, cleaning and rehabilitation, and tenant move-ins and move-outs.

Your best candidate for maintenance coordinator will have a background in construction, plumbing, or electrical work—or will at least understand various elements of these areas. Someone who has filled a "handyman"-type role is often ideal, as they have a broad understanding of issues that will come up and how to fix them. Much like your accounting whiz, they should also be focused on the details, highly process-oriented, and extremely well organized.

Since they'll also be working with every party your business engages with—landlords, tenants, and contractors—thick skin is a must in this role too.

As your business grows, you will find that the maintenance issues never cease. Something somewhere will always be broken, and properties, tenants, and landlords will continually turn over. For these reasons, it's essential that you hire the right person and monitor their workload so you will be aware when the person becomes "maxed out" and requires an assistant. In fact, you should intervene before they reach the point of burnout. Otherwise, any support you provide will be too little too late.

How many accounts is too many? Typically, one person can handle around one hundred accounts. If you have some economies of scale and outsource some tasks to part-timers or virtual assistants, that number might top out around 150–200 accounts.

From the beginning, you must also support your maintenance coordinator with software that accepts, dispatches, and tracks all your inbound maintenance requests. You will pay extra for those software capabilities, but—believe me—they'll be worth it to you and your team. We found them to be game changers. In our business, these systems do the work of two people, resulting in nearly flawless organization and major cost savings.

Home In on the Right People

We've already discussed how difficult property management roles are, but as you're considering whom to employ, you must understand why grit is so important and take it into account during the hiring process. Don't get me wrong, being a salesperson in real estate requires a tremendous amount of grit too. But rewards—and happiness—are also inherent to the process. You're selling the American dream, and thus both joy and gratitude are inevitable. Further, when there are pain points—a seller has to give up a house they've made a lifetime of memories in, or a buyer's bid isn't accepted—they typically don't channel their anger toward you.

Not so in property management. When the phone rings, something's usually wrong. The problem they're calling about is never sexy or glamorous—in fact, it may even be pretty gross. And the people on the receiving end usually bear the brunt of frustration from tenants and landlords alike.

To deal with the onslaught, those in property management must have the unflappable mentality of an MMA fighter. They have to train well and know their stuff backward and forward—all while preparing to get the stuffing kicked out of them from time to time. I don't mean to sound barbaric; that's just how it is.

So how do you find the right people for some of the most challenging jobs there are?

First, you have to attract them—which requires an excellent culture. Create the kind of environment people want to be in, one they know will support them during challenging situations—whether personal or professional.

Next, you should always be looking for talent, as high quality hires are the way to grow. When those résumés start coming in, begin with a thorough background check on promising candidates. When it comes to the interview process, you've got to be thorough. A question about how they dealt with the most difficult situation in their life will provide valuable insight. Knowing the pressure they'll be under, surface-level answers just won't cut it. If someone doesn't have the ability or desire to deal with adversity, this isn't the job for them. Here, things big and small go wrong all the time—and houses catch fire and flood, construction projects hit major snags, toilets clog, squirrels move in uninvited, and more, sometimes all at the same time.

With that in mind, walk them through some of the scenarios they may experience on a daily or weekly basis. Ask, for example, how they might handle a landlord or tenant taking an aggressive approach when they're unsatisfied with a particular outcome and telling them they didn't do their job—even when they know they did. Questions like this one can help you grasp how they'd tackle real-life situations. Do they have the ability to address the issues that will undoubtedly arise, or does it seem like they'll shut down at the first sign of struggle?

Once you understand their experience and approach, inquire about their motivation. Ask them why they want to do this work. What drives them to do this job?

Finally, be frank. Sugarcoating the challenge ahead won't do anyone any favors. Be up front about how difficult their role will be, and ask them if they think they can endure it day in and day out. If you have any hesitations about whether they're being completely honest or know what they're getting themselves into, don't ignore them! Don't hire just to fill a void. Hiring the wrong person now just to fill the seat will only cause you stress down the line.

Find the Best—and Treat Them That Way

It is not an overstatement to say that the success of your management company will depend upon the quality of these first three hires. Select them with utmost care, and train them thoroughly so they have the information to manage whatever's thrown their way. Give them the support they will need to succeed in their jobs—roles that are more difficult than most. Empathize with the challenges they're grappling with on a daily basis. Acknowledge their hard work, because no one else will, thanking them consistently for what is often a thankless job.

Last but not least, take care of your team. Compensate them well. Good people are hard to find in this industry, and burnout rates are high. In addition to offering competitive salaries, we bonus our team based on profitability, celebrate accomplishments with team dinners, and provide additional support on a case-by-case basis. We've helped employees buy much-needed vehicles and pay for vacations, and we do what we can to support their families when necessary.

This job is stressful enough. Enabling your team to rest easy when it comes to their personal life is the right thing to do—and it will help them tune out anything happening at home and focus on the task at hand when they walk through your doors. Your investment will pay off in the form of security, stability, and success.

Next, let's talk about the essential documents that will make their jobs—and yours—easier, namely agreements and leases.

Key Insights

- There are three key hires you'll need to make, ideally at the outset of your business: an accounting whiz, a business development associate or leasing director, and a maintenance coordinator. Each role requires a different skill set, but all of them require grit.

- Your accounting person should be a diligent, highly organized "numbers person." They will handle many financial tasks and should avoid the distraction of dealing with the public.

- Initially, your business development associate or leasing director will bring in new accounts and help with leasing. They should be an excellent salesperson who will track down leads and follow up as needed. Look for someone who is tenacious, has strong marketing instincts, and has the grit and skills to manage the problems that will inevitably arise.

- Your maintenance coordinator will oversee all operations related to repairs, inspections, cleaning and rehabilitation, move-ins, and move-outs. They should understand the construction process, be organized and process-oriented, and be capable of focusing on details. The person must also be able to perform well under stress.

- Be aware of your employees' workloads, and be prepared to hire additional help before they become burned out.

- Choose powerful software that will accept and track inbound maintenance requests.

- Treat your team well. This is a tough business, and you must convey that you understand that. Compensate them fairly, support their needs, and thank them for their contributions so they know how much you value them.

CHAPTER 5

AGREEMENTS

If you're going to enter the property management business, you've got to know your way around property management agreements (PMAs), as they're important and protective tools of the trade. Property management agreements spell out very specifically your company's responsibilities versus those of the landlord and include language that will shield your business from liability when disputes arise—particularly disputes between landlord and tenant, two essential features that help support smooth operations.

To make sure you're covered, regardless of what comes up (and by now you know that includes a diversity of issues, from the ordinary to the supernatural), property management agreements must be both extensive and specific. Here, we'll talk about the elements you should touch on to make sure you're protected.

It's important to note that, no matter how confident you feel after reading this chapter, this is not the time to fly solo and draft your own template agreement or pull one off the internet. Hire a knowledgeable attorney to draft these and other protective measures into a customized document that will address your company's specific needs. A carefully written property management agreement will not only serve as a legal safeguard, but it will also forestall time-wasting arguments, make your processes crystal clear, and help you run a more efficient business—a triple win, if there ever was one.

Before we go any further, it is extremely important to understand that I'm not providing you with legal advice here; I'm simply offering very broad but helpful insights based on my experiences and that of my team. Note, too, that laws in states, counties, and municipalities vary greatly, so it is imperative that you seek legal counsel from a knowledgeable expert familiar with your area and create a completely custom agreement. The same goes for leases, which we'll cover in the next chapter.

What Every Property Management Agreement Should Include

While a standard, off-the-shelf agreement is never the way to go, there are a few key elements that should be a part of your property management agreement no matter what, albeit tailored to your operation. Let's run through the following list, which details the items you need and some of the elements unique to our business:

1. **Your leasing commission, management fee, and the term of the agreement.** To avoid any issues, your leasing commission, management fee, and the term of the agreement

must be clearly delineated from the start. Otherwise, if any type of disagreement arises, you don't have a leg to stand on. While people have good intentions—for the most part— when it comes to money, if you don't have their commitment in writing, you're going to have a problem. Time and time again, our documents have saved us in this department.

So often, landlords question aspects of our operation because they didn't pay attention when we were explaining the agreement. With everything in writing, we can simply direct them back to the paperwork. For example, since we collect the first month's rent as our leasing commission, the management fee for the first month comes out of the second month's rent—

Time and time again, our documents have saved us in this department.

resulting in two management fee charges during the second month. If a landlord were to question why we deducted twice as much money that month, we can simply direct them to their agreement and explain that they signed it, thus confirming they understood the terms.

Curious about our fees and typical agreement lengths? We withhold the entire first month's rent as our leasing commission. Thereafter, we keep 10 percent of the monthly rent as our management fee. Our standard property management agreement term is one year. Renewals usually occur automatically when the tenant's lease is up.

I've said it before, but it bears repeating: as you establish your fees, remember that property management is a tough job and that individual accounts don't provide a huge return. If you don't charge enough per account, you'll actually lose money in the long run—even if your low prices seem to help you net customers up front.

By the same token, the work you do is valuable, and if you

perform well, customers will be willing to pay a premium for your services. Plus, as we established previously, landlords who are looking for the cheapest option will put up roadblocks every step of the way as you try to manage their accounts. So don't be the cheapest in your market. If you provide value, you should get paid for that value. Charge what you're worth.

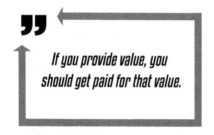

If you provide value, you should get paid for that value.

To do that, you must reverse engineer your pricing. Determine the amount of staff time and resources a particular number of accounts will take and work backward. Taking a month's worth of rent as your leasing commission and 10 percent of the rent each month should be the minimum you charge. Go below that and you'll struggle to run a sound business—and find yourself in a race to the bottom.

If landlords tell you they can get your services at a lower rate, ask them if they're sure they're comparing apples to apples. What services are they getting from the other companies? We often pose that question and find that landlords who shop around and consider what others offer almost always come back.

I also ask those looking for a lower price whether they search for the cheapest financial advisor to manage their money, a doctor to conduct a major procedure, or an attorney to handle a significant business issue. The answer, of course, is "no." I then explain that we provide a service similar to those professionals. We're managing a very expensive asset. Choose the cheapest property management company, and you'll get the cheapest service in exchange. Most people with business acumen will understand that argument.

2. **Indemnity language.** Your attorney's goal will be to indemnify your company against all liability claims, including

those arising from problems that are both beyond and within your control.

Let's say you hire a contractor—someone whom you've worked with before and whose work has never posed any issues. But one time they slip up, missing something that creates a problem (we're all human, after all). Indemnity language provides you with a level of protection. While it can't stop someone from suing you, it does state that taking that action doesn't really matter, as the other party has already agreed that you're indemnified in situations like these.

The language in your agreement should also aim to exclude you from any type of lawsuit between the landlord and the tenant, stressing that your company's only role is to provide management services.

3. **Security deposit disclaimer.** This section should state that the landlord, not your management company, makes all decisions related to security deposits. Indicate that your sole responsibility in such matters is to provide information to the landlord. Here again, you are trying to avoid being pulled into landlord-tenant disputes—you're saying that, since you're not making the decision, you can't be held liable.

Countless times, tenants have attempted to bring us into a lawsuit regarding their security deposit. Every time, we simply reference our property management agreement and our lease (more on that in the next chapter), both of which state that the argument over the security deposit is between tenant and landlord, not us. Further, the indemnity language I just mentioned keeps us out of hot water, since it essentially states that we're not a party to the dispute. On paper and everywhere else, we're just the go-between.

Keep in mind that, while the language and statements in your agreement provide protection, you should never go too far when it comes to influencing the landlord's decision regarding the security deposit. Your role is simply to provide all the information they need to make their own decision—including the laws in your state.

Tenants don't have to be experts in landlord-tenant law to build a viable case against a landlord who holds on to their security deposit. Between their move-in and move-out inspection documentation and the lease itself, they often have enough evidence to successfully sue. We've had landlords disregard the information we provided about what they can and can't charge for, only to be sued and lose. That outcome inevitably costs them much more than the $1,500 or $2,000 they were trying to hold on to via the security deposit. In some states, landlords could wind up paying three times the original security deposit amount, plus legal fees. That's yet another reason to stay out of it.

4. **The landlord's insurance responsibilities.** Remember this: if something bad happens, a plaintiff will typically go after the party with the most money. If your company happens to have more funds than the property owner, you can fully expect to be named in the lawsuit. As such, require that the landlord have appropriate forms of insurance and that they name you as an additional insured party on the policies to serve as an extra layer of protection.

5. **Your administrative fee.** If you choose to charge an administrative fee—a small amount to establish an account and get things up and running—state the required amount, describe the services it covers, and stipulate when the fee is collected. That way, no one can say they didn't know the fee was part of the deal.

6. **Inspections.** State when you will inspect the property to

avoid additional requests for the service. We agree to do move-in and move-out inspections only. At times, we will conduct interim inspections under certain conditions, such as when we hear rumors of overoccupancy or that a tenant has a dog in a pet-free building; however, we do not bind ourselves to those in our agreement.

7. **Your authority to order certain repairs.** Specify that you have carte blanche authority to, first, order any repair projected to cost less than $500 and, second, order any emergency repair. Thus, for example, if a water heater bursts at 3:00 a.m., you can order the replacement without calling the landlord.

In cases where the landlord will authorize a repair, specify that you will need to present only one bid for their consideration, not two or three or four. Why are these stipulations important? To do otherwise would slow the repair process and reflect poorly on your customer service. Tenants expect a quick response, and you can't provide that when you're haggling with the landlord over an essential item.

Each statement I've mentioned here will save you countless hours and allow you to take action as needed without interference, thus providing all parties with a better property management experience.

8. **Repairs related to health and safety.** Reserve the right to unilaterally order the repair of any problem that could potentially threaten a person's health or safety. This clause will protect you and your tenants if an obstinate landlord refuses to consent to the repair.

While we do query the landlord first, if we find that the person doesn't want to "play ball" with us and take the steps to keep their tenants safe, we later terminate the account. Say you find a major structural issue at a particular property, a broken heating system, faulty septic system, major electrical issue, or a leaky roof, for example— something that needs to be replaced, rather than repaired. If it could not only cause serious damage to the home but also endanger the tenants, it must be remedied right away. Those landlords who refuse to take appropriate steps to address it put you—and their tenants—in a dangerous position, and to run a sound business, you just can't let that fly.

9. **Indemnification against problems caused by contractors.** There's another party from which you must shield yourself in the property management game: contractors. Indemnify your company against any defaults or mistakes committed by your company or the contractors you hire. Also state that you make no representation of warranties or guarantees (though you should always make certain that all contractors are licensed and properly insured to avoid any problems up front).

10. **Disclosures required of the landlord.** To manage a property properly, you have to have all the information on it from the start. Your property management agreement should require the landlord to produce, up front, any documents related to a governing HOA or condo association. Also require that the landlord make you aware of anything abnormal or problematic about the property. To that end, we insist that all our landlords complete a disclosure form.

11. **Indemnification from problems related to mold or moisture.** Don't fail to protect your company from any litigation related to these potentially catastrophic problems.

One time, a tenant tried to sue us, claiming that there was mold in the house she was renting and that it was making her sick. We soon found out that she had caused the mold by putting cardboard boxes in the basement, near a faucet that she always left running. In short, the mold was her fault. And because our paperwork clearly stated which actions could cause a problem with moisture, as well as her responsibility to report any issues immediately, we were entirely protected. If we didn't have that paperwork in place, we would have had a real issue on our hands.

12. **Sale of property to the tenant.** State that if the landlord sells the property to the tenant, you are owed 6 percent commission. This will prevent the landlord from going around you to negotiate independently with the tenant.

This is especially important in a competitive real estate market like the one we're in today, as inventory is limited and landlord-tenant sales are common. Commission from these transactions can become a significant stream of income, and documenting it in your property management agreement ensures you can enforce this term if necessary.

You've probably noticed a key theme by now, one that applies to property management operations and virtually every other type of organization: you have to protect yourself to run a good business.

13. **Management fees due for life of the lease.** Suppose you find and fill a vacancy with a great tenant. Then, the landlord comes to you three months into a lease and says, "I want to terminate my management agreement with you, but I'm going to keep the tenant." They think that, because the tenants are so responsive and respectful, they don't need your management services—believing that they can manage the tenant on their own and save themselves your fee. You can avoid situations like these by ensuring that your property management agreement states that you are entitled to receive

management fees for the life of the lease, provided that you found the tenant.

With that clause built in, when landlords come to us and say they plan to handle management for the life of the lease, we simply say, "That's fine with us. There are nine months left on the lease; would you like us to take the remainder of our fee out of the next month's rent?" When they check the paperwork, they have no choice but to acknowledge the terms of the agreement and proceed accordingly.

This element of our agreement proved to be invaluable when navigating a situation with a 180-unit apartment complex we were managing. About a year and a half into our three-year term, new owners acquired the complex. They let us know that, due to the way their funding and financing were set up, they would have to handle property management themselves going forward.

That was okay with us, as the agreement stipulated that we would be paid our fee for the duration of the property management agreement's term. Because our attorneys had ensured our i's were dotted and t's crossed via the property management agreement, we had no problems collecting.

With a larger complex like this one, such stipulations are particularly important, as so much investment capital and infrastructure goes into the front end of the project. As the property manager, you actually make more money later on, since the vast majority of your costs come out at the beginning. In this case, we had allocated significant staff time and resources to the project, and it was gratifying to know we wouldn't lose money for our efforts.

14. **Marketing fee.** It's possible that a landlord may change their mind and decide not to rent a property after you have spent time and money preparing to list and market the home. In such cases, we charge a marketing fee for our efforts.

Otherwise, we lose out on our investment. Specify the fee in your property management agreement so you don't find yourself in a situation where you've inadvertently worked for free.

15. **Right to terminate.** Any marriage can be a challenge, and that extends to your long-term relationships with landlords. There may be times when there's just no other option but divorce. With that in mind, specify in your property management agreement that your company has the right to terminate an agreement at any time, without incurring liability.

Further state that your company will be entitled to compensation beyond the termination date. Though, in cases like these, it's important to determine whether going after the funds you are owed is worth your time and energy. You're likely terminating because the relationship was untenable to begin with, and if there's only $1,500 or $2,000 left on your contract, it may not be worth your effort to go after it.

16. **Lead paint.** Lead paint can pose an expensive problem that many landlords don't want to deal with. Make it clear that it is the responsibility of the landlord to comply with any applicable laws or regulations governing lead paint.

Moreover, it is the landlord's job, not yours, to arrange and pay for testing and mitigation. Require also that the landlord produce certificates proving compliance, so you have proof that they followed through with their end of the bargain.

17. **County and municipal codes.** Similarly, state that the landlord must comply with all applicable county or municipal codes, and that compliance is their responsibility. Caution: never place a noncompliant property on the rental

market. Why? If the municipality finds that the property isn't compliant, you'll be given a certain period of time to rectify the situation. If you don't, they'll condemn the property and evict the tenants, and you'll find yourself stuck.

We make sure we never find ourselves in this situation by conducting an initial inspection and checking for compliance before a tenant moves in. In cases in which we catch an issue in a property that's already occupied, we tell the landlord it must be fixed. And if they don't follow through, that's grounds for termination.

18. **Disbursement date.** Specify a date on which or by which the landlord will be paid (for example, on the tenth of the month or by the tenth of the month).

As I mentioned, one of our claims to fame is that we are fast payers, but whether or not you can provide a super quick turnaround, it's still beneficial for landlords to know when they can expect their money. Doing so will prevent your team from fielding unnecessary calls as landlords try to track down their funds. Just make sure to be realistic and choose a date that you can manage.

19. **Legal fees.** This one is extremely important. State that the landlord will be responsible for your company's legal costs if you are named in a lawsuit as a result of the landlord's negligence.

Suppose, for example, that one of your landlords wants to fight a tenant over a security deposit. The landlord might have second thoughts after considering that they might be on the hook for your company's legal fees if you are dragged into a lawsuit.

20. **Affiliated businesses.** Have your attorney do your affiliated business disclosures in compliance with RESPA—which we will talk about more later. Any financial interest you have

in any company must be disclosed. Disclose in your PMA and your lease any financial relationships that you have with contractors or other professionals who may provide services for your landlord and tenant. When we discuss this matter with our landlords, we always cast our association with these businesses as a benefit, noting, for example, that a tenant's request for a repair flows more efficiently through our system when we are able to use our own contractor.

21. **Owner accounting portal.** Specify in the PMA how the landlord will receive statements and other accounting information. When a landlord signs with us, we set the person up with a web-based "owner portal," where they can view expenses, income, invoices for repairs, and other transactions at any time. Making such information freely available to our landlords also benefits us. Why? We receive fewer phone inquiries—"Hey, where's my rent?" or "What was this bill for?"

They don't have to ask, since it's all in the system.

In the previous chapter, we talked about the necessity of using software designed for property managers. Our choice, AppFolio, powers the owner portals mentioned here.

22. **Evictions.** Staying within the boundaries of state law, fully describe your eviction process. Also state that the property owner is responsible for any court costs related to eviction, and that the decision to evict lies solely with your management company. This is important because sometimes a landlord will want to "work with" a delinquent tenant who has been in the residence for a long time. Our experience tells us that following the law of the state and filing an eviction

as soon as it's legally allowable stops repeat offenders before they start.

For this reason, we file eviction papers on the first day allowed by our state laws. That way, the case will be placed on that month's docket. Filing later means your case could be pushed to the following month, putting the tenant two months behind on their rent—rather than just one.

Ultimately, it's the landlord's decision, but you must explain the potential ramifications of failing to enforce the law when the tenant doesn't pay. If a landlord wants to continue working with the tenant anyway, then *you* have a business decision to make. Do you want to work with someone who doesn't heed your professional advice?

23. **Late fee policy.** Specify that your company retains 100 percent of any late fees collected. Some landlords don't like this policy, but we feel that we earn the money incurred via late fees, since we typically spend so much time aggressively chasing after that late-paying tenant. The good news: late fees can be a significant source of income for your company. We collect six figures in late fees each year.

Alterations to Your Property Management Agreement

Just like everything else in life, your property management business will change, and you'll need to adjust your property management agreement to keep up. As your business grows and you acquire more experience, you and your attorney will continue to add language to your agreements. Our property management agreement documents (we use different versions, depending on the type of account) generally run from nine to eleven pages in length. Meanwhile, our competitors' PMAs are typically just one or two pages long.

With that in mind, consider all the important contingencies that we cover that they don't! With so much left undefined and open to chance, they can't possibly be properly protected from the commonplace issues that occur in our field. You have the chance to shield yourself from the start.

Since we take such care in preparing these documents, you probably won't be surprised to learn that we don't allow a landlord to make any changes whatsoever to an agreement—no scratch-outs, no expanded paragraphs.

The only exception would involve a landlord who is willing to bring us a great number of accounts. Since our standard property management agreement is written primarily for a landlord with one or two properties, we would have our attorney draft a customized agreement for the owner of, say, twenty or thirty homes. Even in this case, however, we wouldn't budge on the language related to liability and indemnification. Property management is a difficult business, and we managers need to protect ourselves.

Follow Fair Housing Guidelines

We include a fair housing rider in all our agreements—a federally mandated addition. To avoid any potential accusations related to discrimination, we also outsource our tenant-selection process. We send data on our potential tenants to a third-party company, which then rates the applicants simply as "pass" or "fail" based on their credit rating.

Our screening process was designed by our legal team to be compliant with fair housing, and we suggest you take a similar approach, working with an attorney in a formal capacity to ensure you're following the fair housing process as it relates to renting to tenants. That way, it's just a numbers game; subjectivity doesn't factor into it. Additionally, make sure to share this policy with all potential owners.

It's important to note, too, that protected classes vary from state to state, something that should be taken into account during each of your transactions. This is yet another reason why it's crucial to work with an attorney who can walk you through your state's guidelines.

The bottom line here? Your property management agreements should protect you in full, regardless of what comes up. Thorough documentation that you can refer to in any number of situations will provide you with peace of mind, prevent you from being pulled into any unnecessary lawsuits, and help you enforce fees and dictate responsibilities as necessary.

Next, we'll talk about leases, the tenant-focused complement you need to ensure you're completely covered.

Key Messages

- Your property management agreement should specify your leasing commission, your management fee, and the term of the agreement.

- In preparing your property management agreement, your attorney's goal should be to indemnify your company against all liability claims.

- Insert language that will exclude you from any disputes arising between the landlord and tenant, including disagreements related to security deposits.

- Establish that your company has the right, under certain circumstances, to order repairs without first obtaining permission from the landlord.

- Disclose any financial relationships you may have with contractors. Disclaim any responsibility for defaults or mistakes caused by contractors whom you hire.

- State the landlord's responsibilities. Require that they disclose any problems related to the property. Where applicable, also require copies of condo or HOA rules.

- Require a 6 percent commission if the landlord sells the property to the tenant.

- Specify any payments that may be due to you following termination of the property management agreement.

- Establish that it is the landlord's responsibility to do whatever is necessary to place the building in compliance with all applicable laws, regulations, and codes—including those related to lead paint.

- Describe how and when you will pay the landlord and how you will provide accounting information.

- Declare that the landlord will be responsible for your legal costs if your company is named in a lawsuit due to the landlord's negligence.

- Fully describe your eviction process and establish with your landlord up front that in your professional opinion, you need to file eviction at the earliest time your state allows to avoid potential issues later. State that the landlord will be responsible for any related court costs.

- Specify the percentage of late fees that your company will retain (we collect 100 percent).

- With few exceptions, do not allow a landlord to alter your property management agreement.

- Avoid potential fair-housing challenges by outsourcing the process of approving or disapproving tenant applications.

CHAPTER 6

LEASES

You've heard the warning innumerable times: "Put everything in writing. " And so it goes with leases. Rather than hammering out the details with landlords, leases clarify the roles and responsibilities that belong to you and those that belong to tenants. The document, which your tenants will sign, must spell out with exacting specificity their responsibilities and yours, including what will take place if problems or disputes arise.

Put everything in writing.

In this chapter, I'll run through some of the hot topics that your lease must carefully address—and what happens if you fail to dictate this stuff up front. Keep in mind that your lease's language can never be too specific. The more details you include, the better. You just can't overdo it.

Also recognize that, just as with a property management agreement, an "off-the-shelf" lease purchased on the internet or at a box store will not suffice. Your lease must be a custom job, prepared by an attorney who is well versed in landlord-tenant law.

But there's an upside to all this paperwork: the time, money, and effort you spend preparing a proper lease now will undoubtedly save you money, headaches, and time in the future.

As we mentioned in the previous chapter, there are all kinds of legal nuances in every state when it comes to landlord tenant law. Again, these are just broad suggestions that have helped us thrive in the property management business. Please make sure that the agreement you come up with is drafted by an attorney with expertise in landlord-tenant law.

What Every Lease Should Include

Here's a thorough list of your lease must-haves:

1. **General indemnity clause**. Identify your company as the property manager and state that your firm is to be held harmless in any disputes arising between the landlord and the tenant (flip back to the previous chapter for more on why indemnity language is so important).

2. **Security deposits.** State that your company is to be held harmless in any landlord-tenant disputes concerning security deposits. Following state guidelines, explain your process for returning or retaining security deposit money. List problems and items that the tenant could be charged for should issues arise and specify what the remedial costs will be. We include

a detailed account of potential costs, from cleaning to repairs. That takes the guesswork out of it. We also make sure that our estimates are on the higher end (and we provide these to tenants as examples of what they could be charged for and what to possibly expect from a cost perspective) to account for variations in the market and ensure there are no surprises.

You should also enumerate what the tenant's closing responsibilities will be at exit time. For example, we require that the tenant have the unit professionally cleaned (including steam cleaning the carpets) prior to their departure. We also require that the tenant pay the last water and sewer bill, and, in the case of oil or gas heat, replenish the tank to the level present at move-in.

3. **Utilities.** List any utilities that the renter will be required to cover. Be careful here. If your state does not allow a tenant's name to be placed on a utility account, the tenant may claim that they are not responsible for paying the bills. Forestall that problem with a paragraph to the contrary. This is very important!

Early on, as we took over accounts and portfolios, we found that leases were unclear about who was responsible for each utility. For example, the landlord might be paying gas and electric bills under his name while expecting to be reimbursed by the tenants. But because the utility responsibilities weren't specified in the lease, the landlord was having trouble collecting.

Meanwhile, if your state permits an account to be listed in a tenant's name, state in your lease that the tenant must place the account in their name *before* moving in.

4. **Disclosure concerning ancillary companies.** If applicable, disclose in both your lease and your property management

agreement that you and your management company have a financial relationship with certain companies that may perform repairs and other services at the property.

5. **Late payments.** Following state law, describe when a rent payment will be considered late and disclose what the late charge will be. We strictly enforce our late fees, as you know!

6. **Breach of lease/evictions.** Include aggressive language on these topics. Let tenants know that if they breach the lease, an eviction will follow. Then, specify your eviction process, making sure that it complies with state mandates. If an eviction becomes necessary, follow your process precisely.

I live near a university, where students occupy many of the houses near campus. They often don't realize how strict and serious we are about overoccupancy—which counts as a breach of lease and violates the municipality's rules. Often, it's the municipality that will step in and force additional tenants out or condemn the house. Our lease policy also requires that those occupying a residence must also be on the lease, another common issue in college towns. Thus, we make these factors abundantly clear in our paperwork and describe the eviction process that will unfold if tenants don't comply.

7. **HOA and condo rules.** When applicable, state that the tenant must follow all condo and HOA rules and that failure to do so will be grounds for eviction. Attach a copy of the rules to the lease, so there's no question about the rules.

8. **Pets.** State your pet policy. If pets are allowed and you charge a pet fee, indicate whether the fee is refundable or nonrefundable.

9. **Anything out of the ordinary.** Is there something about a

specific property that needs to be addressed? Don't hesitate to put it in writing (for example, in an addendum). Remember, property management is a litigious business, and overlooking a particular detail will only hurt you in the year.

10. **Lease renewal/termination.** Clearly define the term of the lease and explain what will happen when the term nears its conclusion.

In our case, all our leases require that the tenant provide sixty days' notice as to whether they will renew or vacate (we query the tenant about ninety days before the lease is set to expire). If a tenant fails to provide sixty days' notice and stays beyond the lease's termination date, the lease will renew automatically and the tenant will need to give us, at minimum, an additional sixty days' notice before exiting. A tenant who fails to respond at all to our query could be considered a "held-over tenant" if they stay beyond the lease's expiration, and an eviction process will ensue.

Before we query the tenant, we naturally contact the property owner to determine their intentions. The owner may wish to continue to rent the property, or they may wish to sell.

The key here is that we follow a predetermined renewal/exit process and that we explain that process in writing to our tenants. In doing so, we try to avoid surprises, such as a last-minute phone call from a renter who says, "Well, okay, I want to move."

11. **Tenant versus landlord responsibilities.** Specify any task for which the tenant is responsible and any task that will fall upon the landlord, HOA, or condo association. Responsibilities might include cutting the lawn, raking leaves, removing snow, power washing the building, changing water or HVAC filters, or repairing broken appliances. One way to document

these obligations is to include side-by-side check-off lists showing who does what and/or who pays for what. That way, when something breaks, we can simply return to our list and explain whose responsibility it is.

In some cases, you may also need to insert a clause or two to cover a special situation. For example, in the case of our student rentals, some parents elect to pay us to cut the grass so that their children can avoid that particular chore.

12. **Service call charges for which the tenant would be required to pay.** Include in the lease any service call circumstance that would require payment by the tenant.

Here's an example: Some of our landlords require that their tenants periodically change the HVAC filter. If the system were to fail as a result of an unchanged filter, the tenant would have to pay for the service call.

We also state how much it will cost if we have to make an unnecessary maintenance call, like sending out a vendor to flip a breaker—an expense we can't pass on to the homeowner.

Thanks to our AppFolio software system, a specialist in a maintenance call center actually walks the tenant through a series of preliminary questions when the tenant calls to register a problem, such as, "Have you checked the breaker?" When they claim they have, and a vendor arrives only to find that they didn't do what they said, we have plenty of documentation to show that they initiated an unnecessary call.

The AppFolio service has proven invaluable to us. Because every call is recorded and documented in the system, we don't find ourselves in the sticky situations that can so easily arise if and when someone misses a step.

13. **Certified funds.** Require that your tenants pay their first month's rent by certified funds before they move in. In the past, we've accepted checks, allowed tenants to take possession, and then discovered a few days later that the checks were no good. When that happened, we were faced with evicting new arrivals—a costly and tedious process—only to have to fill the vacancy again. Save yourself the pain.

14. **Renter's insurance.** Require that tenants purchase renter's insurance (and that they show proof of insurance) before they can move in. Frankly, renter's insurance is inexpensive, and it can be a lifesaver for a renter if a catastrophe—a flood or fire, for example—destroys the person's personal property, so this investment is truly in their best interest.

By the same token, requiring renter's insurance also protects you and the property owner. Let's say that the tenant allows their insurance to lapse, subsequently suffers damages in the home, and then tries to sue you and the owner. If you can show that the tenant failed to keep the insurance in force in violation of the lease, you and the owner will have a stronger defense against the suit.

Enforcement

If you are to run a really well-oiled "property management machine," you *must* enforce the requirements and prohibitions included in your lease. Evictions, late fees, breach of lease, noise violations—do not overlook such things. Of course, we're all human. Most of us want to help others by nature. But it doesn't benefit you to bend the rules for tenants who are likely attempting to game the system.

You can't walk into an Apple store and tell them you want to pay

$800 for an iPhone that costs $1,200. The "geniuses" would laugh at you. The same should be true for your company. Remember that you have to protect yourself to run a sound business, follow your documented remedial processes, and "do what needs to be done."

Additional Documents

I mentioned earlier that, when applicable, we provide our tenants with a copy of any condo or HOA rules. We also provide a copy of our move-in inspection and a list of any necessary repairs that we have identified. In addition, we furnish our tenants with a "welcome packet" that includes all our maintenance phone numbers, as well as a description of which numbers apply to which types of problems. Also in the packet are the instructions and logins, for which they will need to set up an account on our online portal. That way, they have all the tools they need to fulfill their end of the bargain.

Verbally Explain Your Documents and Processes

Good communication is the cornerstone of any effective agreement.

Good communication is the cornerstone of any effective agreement. Before move-in, your leasing agent should walk the tenant through the most important features of the lease and its accompanying documents. At a minimum, the agent should explain:

- the inspection processes (prior to move-in and following move-out),

- how you manage security deposits (explain the process fully and make sure that the language in your lease is airtight),

- what utilities and other expenses the tenant must pay,

- how the renewal/exit process works,

- how and where to call for maintenance, and

- what to do in an emergency.

The better your agent explains these elements, the more likely you will avoid bottlenecks, hassles, and legal challenges in the future.

Your First Steps

So how do you go about crafting an effective lease? First and foremost, study the landlord-tenant laws and regulations in your state. Then, hire an attorney (perhaps on retainer) who specializes in property management. Have them draft your lease, paying attention to the items which I have mentioned here. Also ask the attorney to explain to you any sections of the lease that you don't fully understand upon receipt.

You can learn from my mistakes. When we first started, we used boilerplate leases and property management agreements. Several costly mistakes and headaches later, we took the time and spent the money to get our documents right. Ultimately, it was a small expense up front that saved us a lot of time, effort, and liability down the line.

Taking these steps not only protects your company but also protects the rights of your tenants and property owners.

Finally, recognize that a thorough, well-written lease will promote efficiency; avoid, resolve, or eliminate many problems; and ultimately allow you to spend your time and energy as they should be spent—toward the process of building and expanding your company.

Key Messages

- Hire an attorney who is well versed in landlord-tenant law to prepare your lease.

- Include language that indemnifies your company from disputes arising between the landlord and the tenant.

- Describe in detail your security deposit policies and procedures. Provide examples of problems that would debit the tenant's account. Specify the costs of correcting those problems.

- Fully explain when a tenant will be charged a late-payment fee. Specify the fee.

- Firmly state your eviction and breach-of-lease policies. Strictly enforce these policies.

- If applicable, provide copies of HOA or condo rules. Explain that failure to follow them could result in eviction.

- Define the term of the lease and describe the renewal/exit process.

- Specify the tenant's responsibilities versus the landlord's responsibilities.

- Describe the circumstances under which a tenant would be required to pay for a service call.

- Require that the tenant pay the first month's rent in certified funds. If it's appropriate for your market, require online rent payments.

- Require renter's insurance.

- Prior to move-in, provide copies of your inspection report and your list of potential repairs.

- Offer a welcome packet that lists important phone numbers and any logins that the tenant will need to establish an online account.

- Walk your tenant through the lease and any accompanying documents.

- Recognize that a well-written lease reduces headaches and promotes efficiency and growth.

CHAPTER 7

MARKETING

Which marketing strategies will help me land my first property management accounts?

Which ones will help me scale my business?

How can I reach landlords who own multiple properties?

What should I say when I present to a seasoned landlord?

How do I address the fears of first-time investors?

If you're new to the property management business, you probably have all these questions and then some. There are so many factors to consider, and—especially when you're first getting things up and running—many of them, including the ones mentioned here, come down to marketing.

In this chapter, we'll address these and many other specific questions, all for one purpose, to help you answer a larger question, one you and your property management team will ask yourselves every day: **Which marketing strategies should we use to acquire properties from landlords?**

With that in mind, let's talk about some of the marketing strategies that can serve you as you kick things off—and well into the future.

Leverage What You've Already Learned

Fortunately, the same strategies and forms of media that you have used to build your real estate sales funnel will also prove effective in launching and promoting your property management business. If, for example, you've mastered social media and video, by all means rely on the same tools to announce and build your property management division.

Keep in mind, too, that whatever marketing expertise you bring to your property management company from the sales side of your business will likely help you stand out among your competition. The reason? Most property management companies do a sad job of marketing their services. In fact, many do nothing at all—other than listing their services on the internet. That makes it easy to set yourself apart. If you're already running a solid sales business, complete with effective marketing, you're already halfway there.

Prepare to Launch

Don't open your new business's doors without first telling everyone in your sphere that you're about to enter the property management space. Announce your intentions using social media, your websites, your video channels, and any other platforms that have served you well in real estate sales. You should definitely dive into your databases and send appropriate messages to those who own investment properties and those who might consider purchasing them. Doing so will likely help you secure your first clients.

Don't forget to follow up either. Put together multiple mail pieces and social media ads and blast them out every forty-five to sixty days up until your launch. Once you've had your "opening day," repeat the process, broadcasting that you've arrived forty-five or sixty days afterward.

You should also create a separate website for your property management business. That will allow you to clearly distinguish your property management traffic from your sales traffic. As a result, you will be better able to track and manage both groups. With that said, don't hesitate to link your sales and property management sites. Doing so will promote cross-pollination without affecting your ability to separately track visitors to either site.

Reach Out to Gatekeepers

To rapidly scale your business, focus on finding clients who own multiple properties. Regardless of the number of accounts you're hoping to secure, it's a lot easier to meet your benchmarks when you can pick up a bundle of units at one time. We're happy to find an owner with ten to fifteen accounts, but every so often we get lucky and sign a landlord with sixty, seventy-five, or eighty units. I've found that one way to contact and connect with these owners is through the professionals with whom they regularly do business: lawyers, CPAs, and financial advisors. I refer to these professionals as the owners' "gatekeepers." Because they already have an established relationship with these professionals, owners intrinsically trust their recommendations. Thus, when their lawyer or CPA recommends you as a property manager, owners are often ready and willing to hear what you have to offer. Much of the time, that means you get to skip the sales pitch.

By establishing and nurturing relationships with such people, we've met landlords who have handed us some of our biggest accounts to date. In most cases, these referrals have been for buildings with twenty-five or more units. Remember the large apartment complex I managed and then purchased? The original owner was first referred to me by his CPA. In addition, we've secured hundreds of accounts through real estate attorneys. And just recently, I purchased another fifty-unit building thanks to a connection made through my attorney.

To begin, we simply phoned the gatekeepers and said, "We're getting into the property management business. If you know any property owners, send them our way." Ultimately, we won tons of accounts, but be aware: it didn't happen overnight. We didn't just call each gatekeeper once and cross our fingers, hoping that they'd pass on our information. We established enduring relationships with these folks, and—in many cases—began doing business with them ourselves.

One way to stay in touch with gatekeepers is to place them in your funnel and then target them with some sort of drip campaign. You can also take them to lunch and phone them regularly. Be friendly and consistently remind them that you're in the property management business and that you'd like to help any of their clients who own investment real estate.

If you keep plugging away, in time you'll begin to scale very quickly, and ultimately those referrals will start stacking up.

Launch a Hybrid Plan: Digital Meets Old School

One quick way to win clients is to market directly to real estate investors using your social media channels. I find that the segment of people we reach on social media is often underserved. Here, we typically connect with younger, first-time investors who have grown up on the internet. Many of them are a little gun-shy because they haven't received much of an education on the real estate investment opportunities available to them. Providing basic information about some of the ways in which owning real estate can help them build wealth; defining basic concepts like depreciation, appreciation, and leverage; and more makes a real difference—particularly when they're ready to buy. We frequently share short, two-minute educational videos on Facebook designed to inform those who are intrigued by the possibility of investing in real estate but unsure of where to start.

By making them feel safe about the decision they're considering, you're building trust. That's how you get people to buy from you.

We've recently begun focusing on Instagram as well. Putting out content on investing in real estate, staying motivated, and maintaining a positive mindset has won us tens of thousands of followers and lots of engagement. Sharing stats, quotes, and simple insights in a bullet point format has been extremely effective. We've even had a few short videos go viral. Our experience has shown that there's a huge upside to leveraging digital marketing, specifically when it comes to that next-generation investor. As such, don't hesitate to put effort into socials. Give out valuable information for free, before asking for a sale. Chances are, it will pay off.

A second method, mining your software system for sales contacts, will also help you spread your message. But it's not all about digital.

A third way—one that works far better with property management than it does with sales—is to send direct mail. Don't be afraid of old-school tactics like this one. Many of your potential property management clients are older themselves, and they still pay attention to print media. We've achieved remarkable results with direct mail and now use the medium monthly.

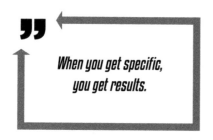

When you get specific, you get results.

Of course, we don't just send out mailings indiscriminately with the hope that a certain percentage of our pieces will find receptive landlords. We use a company called Melissa Data to buy lists of well-targeted property owners. We ask specifically for data sets of owners of two or more properties. We further specify that those properties be nonowner occupied. In the past, we've also requested data on LLCs that owned more than one property. When you get specific, you get results.

To boost our success, we continually refresh our lists, and we strive to produce creative and memorable mailing pieces. One of our best efforts pictured a roulette wheel and carried the headline, "Don't gamble with your property." The copy listed all the services we provide for our landlords, and then, to engage the reader and make the piece more enticing, we inserted a lottery ticket in the mailing. Every month, we would follow up with a mail piece highlighting a different service that we offered, from transparency in billing to 24/7 protection, headache-free maintenance, and more. If we could get email addresses for those individuals, we would follow up with Facebook ads, ensuring they would see us twice, in two different formats.

Our research has also helped us hone our message. We've found that most investors dislike managing their properties. Knowing that rich is measured in dollars and wealth is measured in time, they view those tasks as draining a precious resource. (Potential investors especially fear dealing with maintenance and tenant problems, which can chew up both dollars and hours.) And like all humans, they fear the unknown. *What happens if something goes wrong?* We therefore stress these pain points in our literature—letting our potential clients know that we can lift these burdens from their shoulders. That messaging shows them that we're equipped to address the issues that keep them up at night—which goes a long way. When we speak directly to their needs, they are open to hearing about the service we can provide. In so many cases, we have formed long-term relationships in which investors continue to buy properties without worry, and we continue to manage them.

Business Magazines and Newspapers

You can also find significant success by posting ads in print media. Beyond direct mail, we've also made meaningful connections with landlords by advertising in newspapers and magazines that are specially targeted to businesspeople. Our local Chamber of Commerce newspaper and other local business publications have produced surprisingly strong results, particularly in an age most perceive to be 100 percent digital.

Phone Calls

For many, cold calls seem old school too, but don't be afraid to pick up the phone. We've won accounts time after time by directly phoning multiunit owners. We typically ask, "Who are you in management with? Are you happy?" These simple questions open the door for a conversation.

Unsurprisingly, a lot of these owners tell us that they are *not* happy with their current managers. Their feedback serves as further evidence that a lot of companies manage properties as a side hustle, rather than their business priority. As a result, they provide poor customer service.

By phoning potential clients, we have also learned that we need to persevere in our pursuit of their business. These owners are typically wealthy, savvy businesspeople. They are not going to say "yes" during the first phone call—or even after we deliver the first package. Through our conversations with them, we learned to be tenacious. By contacting them consistently over time, we found that our efforts compounded and led to eventual success. Those insights continue to inform our outreach process today.

Marketing to the Mom-and-Pops

As we researched our market and dug into different strategies, we discovered that a lot of owners were elderly and still managing their own properties. They were the ones responding to late-night phone calls about broken boilers or burst pipes, handling the landscaping, and prepping properties for the next tenant, even though they were well into their golden years.

Oftentimes, they had reached an age at which they no longer wanted to spend the time, effort, and energy required to continue managing their properties. Many of these folks were happy to give us their accounts. In fact, we have won a substantial number of accounts by approaching smaller mom-and-pop property management companies that were actually self-managed—meaning the principals owned and managed mostly their own properties and perhaps some others held by family members.

Typically, the company would handle fifty, seventy-five, or a hundred properties. Very often, when we presented these individuals with plans describing how we would handle their properties, we picked up their business in short order. In fact, approaching the mom-and-pop shops turned out to be a very successful strategy for us.

We also found that younger generations who had inherited properties from their families were interested in our help too. While they wanted the investments, and the residual money they provided, they weren't interested in the headaches of management. When we told them we could take that part off their hands, they were more than happy to work with us. Today, we manage hundreds of these accounts.

Highlight Your Best Services

Of course, you've got to have the right messaging when you do your outreach—whether online, through the mail, or over the phone. Presenting to a property owner is much like presenting at a listing appointment. Be succinct and enumerate the services that you will provide, services such as the following:

Timely payments. Landlords are understandably concerned about when they will receive their rent money. As a manager, you should do all you can to distribute rent money near the *beginning* of each month—not at the end of the month as many managers do. Early payment is such a strong benefit that this service alone will help you beat out your competition and win you numerous accounts.

Professional photos. Usually our potential property management clients have heard of us through our sales business. We ask these landlords if they have seen listings for the properties we have for sale and the beautiful pictures we take. When they say they have, we respond, "Well, we'll do the same thing for your rentals."

Unlike most property management companies, which snap photos with an iPhone, we hire professional photographers to take photos of each property before we list them.

Listing on the MLS. Another element that sets us apart from the competition: we ensure the most exposure possible.

In the past, in Maryland, where our property management business is located, you didn't have to be licensed to be a property manager. Those who weren't licensed couldn't list on the Multiple Listing Services (or MLSs), limiting their exposure. Even though regulations have recently changed, property managers *still* don't list on the MLS. In fact, in our market, we are the *only* company that lists rentals on the MLS, a practice that has a huge impact on our business. And since we have a service agreement through the MLS, our properties automatically upload to Zillow and Trulia.

We explain that benefit to potential clients, sharing that, unlike our competitors, we place our rentals on the MLS, a strategy that enhances visibility by pushing the listing into numerous data feeds.

Additionally, many unlicensed property managers used to be able to list their rentals on Zillow for free, but now Zillow has started charging $10 per week per property. Now that there is a cost involved, many of those managers are posting elsewhere—a decision that further limits their reach.

When you combine those opportunities for exposure with video marketing and social media—efforts that few other property management companies engage in—you'll be sure to stand out from your competition.

Locating tenants. We excel at locating tenants, due in large part to the fact that our policies and procedures are stricter than most. First, we have a robust application process. We prequalify every prospective tenant before any agent goes out to show a property. We require a minimum credit score of 600, no evictions, no repossessions, and no foreclosures in the last seven years. In addition, the candidate's monthly income must be at least three times the rental amount. Those qualifications contribute to the pass-fail score I mentioned previously. Assuming that the candidate passes and wants to rent the property, we then share our information with the homeowner so they can make a decision.

Our strict adherence to the application process—everyone must pay an application fee, everyone on the lease must be on the application, everyone must pass a credit check, and more—has served us well. We have seen other property management companies skip steps, resulting in myriad issues. We don't lower our standards just to collect a commission. Yes, we want to fill the house, but we know that cutting corners will come back to haunt us in the end.

Maintaining a comprehensive process doesn't hinder our ability to find good tenants—just the opposite, in fact. We rent thirty or forty properties each month, which puts us ahead of everyone else and has made us the largest on the Eastern Shore of Maryland.

The move-in/move-out process. A large and important part of our value proposition is our airtight move-in/move-out process. We are not shy about explaining how our process works and why ours is better than everyone else's. We enforce the leases that we sign—unlike many other property management companies, which sign leases that they don't understand or that don't comply with state laws. In fact, when Long & Foster updated its leases, we were part of the process.

In addition, we share that our airtight move-in/move-out inspection process includes more than three hundred pictures of each property and detailed notes, which helps us protect landlords in addition to ourselves, as accurate data is essential if any party is called into court.

You should take a similar tack. Since many potential clients assume that all property management companies are created equal, be ready to articulate your strengths, particularly those that involve infrastructure and procedures that otherwise might not be apparent to the client.

Garner Support Online

Note, too, that you don't have to do all the legwork yourself. Your clients can be your best advocates and boost your business by singing your praises. To that end, don't underestimate the value of online reviews. As you would with sales, do everything you can to get an abundance of positive reviews. Most of the time, if you build it—a great business established on the basic tenets of speaking to their concerns and providing convenience and top-notch customer service—the reviews will come. These will counteract the occasional (but inevitable) negative reviews that your property management company will receive—typically from disgruntled tenants.

Your clients can be your best advocates and boost your business by singing your praises.

While it's definitely not worth it to take these bad reviews personally, you should also have a process in place to respond to them. In most cases, we call the complainer, walk through their issue, and do our part to resolve it. More often than not, we find that the person had a beef that was truly with the landlord, rather than with us, and that they just wanted the space to air their grievances. Sometimes, even a simple conversation is enough to make a bad review go away.

When it comes to sourcing and securing new clients, you can also get creative and find less traditional avenues to pursue.

Student Housing and Requests for Proposals

We have won hundreds of lucrative accounts in our market by going after student housing. We targeted the universities themselves and the investors who are interested in student housing. And one of the things that we learned was not surprising, given our experience in property management at large: most of the companies that serve this niche market don't do a very good job. That meant there was plenty of room for us to penetrate the market, advertising the same systems and features that had served us with traditional residential properties.

Whether you pursue student units in your own market or in a market nearby, another way to break into the segment is by responding to formal requests for proposals (RFPs) issued by property owners or by county, state, or federal agencies. RFPs often appear in newspaper or online ads and frequently originate with county- or state-run economic development bodies. These bodies frequently provide financing for student units and for other government-related housing projects.

I will add that these projects produce market-rate rents and are well worth pursuing. In fact, a student housing account or a state- or federal-backed management account can be extremely lucrative, and, frankly, these properties are not that difficult to manage—no more difficult than, say, a twenty-five- or thirty-unit property that you would obtain through traditional marketing efforts. Just make sure you have the infrastructure and knowledge to handle them. We didn't pursue them until we felt we were truly able to deal with large accounts.

It's also worth noting that many landlords who own more than twenty-five properties prefer to use RFPs when soliciting managers. The landlords expect to see formal, detailed RFPs that specify exactly which services you will provide. Consider this an opportunity rather than just extra work, as articulating your value proposition clearly and concisely on paper brings you one step closer to securing multiple accounts in one fell swoop.

Expired Listings

Another way we've picked up accounts is by sending our property management marketing collateral to expired sales listings. To do that, we simply search for them on the MLS. It's a huge avenue for potential properties, because you'll find properties there that owners want to rent. They just need to know the process. Often the owner will respond, "Yes, I would consider renting my property, but I'm still interested in selling it." We then advise the owner that we could list the property either as a rental or a sale—or we could list it as both, simultaneously, and see what type of offer appears first.

This brings up another point: it's important that you include rental information in your sales listing packets. That will give your agents the option to say up front, "If for some reason your sale doesn't work out and you choose to rent your property, we can offer that service too." Such a suggestion separates you from your competition by signaling to the customer that you are prepared to help in ways that other agents can't. We've come to understand that our rental efforts often lead to sales and vice versa. Be prepared to switch tracks. Remember, yours is a full-service real estate company, and that's uniquely valuable.

The First-Time Investor

Another niche target, for both sales and property management, is the person who has saved some money and is considering investing in real estate for the first time. The key to marketing to this person is to remember their biggest fear: managing the property they purchase. In your copy, in your videos, and on social media, address this fear directly. Ask, "Have you ever thought about getting into real estate but held off due to fears about how you'd manage the property?" Keep in mind, too, that the first-timer is likely to be a little younger than your typical property manager, so digital advertising—rather than direct mail—is a wise choice. And one other point: Since this person doesn't yet own investment property, you won't find them through your normal data searches. Search using the broad net of your proven digital channels.

Follow-Up

Regardless of whom you're trying to reach or the method you're using to connect, follow-up is key. It's often just about hitting a prospective landlord over and over and over again. It typically takes about ten hits by mail before you get a phone call. And the phone call is just the beginning, because typically, when they do call, they're just looking to find out what your fees are.

For owners with more than one account—those that our director of operations, Shane Snoots, refers to as "whales"—you may have ten or fifteen interactions beyond that first call. And we're not just talking about a quick check-in over the phone. These are hours-long sit-downs, lunches, and dinners. You really have to work at these accounts. Remember that these owners are trusting you with what may be their most significant investment—especially since they have multiple properties in their portfolios. Plus, with so many units to manage, you essentially become a part of their team. Thus, nothing happens overnight. You have to consistently follow up to be successful. In fact, these owners will judge you based on how you follow up with them before the deal is even done. They're testing you to see how you're going to treat them after you do get them to sign on the dotted line.

It's also crucial to be aware that they have likely already had a bad experience with another management company. Know, too, that they probably already know the typical fees in the market and the average service level. That makes it your job to tell them what you can do better than your competitors and emphasize how you can help them. Whatever your value proposition is, whatever services you're selling, you give that landlord—that potential client—a glimpse of what their experience with you will be like. That's one of the factors that separates us from our competitors. We communicate our services very clearly to the owner prior to doing business, as you now know.

That brings us to the next stage of the marketing game: truly knowing what your competitors are doing in the market and what they're charging—as well as your value proposition.

Know Your Market—and Share Your Value Proposition

If you're not yet an expert in every area of property management, you'll need to become one. To be successful in this game, you've got to understand capitalization rates, ROIs, cash flow, NOIs—all the things that savvy investors consider when they analyze a property.

You'll also need to know your market, including the best places to buy rentals, where there's great cash flow, where the emerging markets are, and where there's strong upside. Translate and share this information with all your investors—the old pros and the first-timers alike. Doing so is just another way to set yourself apart from the typical agent. Frankly, not many agents are very knowledgeable about the investment side of our business, and when you show landlords that you truly understand the elements that affect them, they'll trust you to manage their most important asset.

Next, you've got to make the case for your operation and what you can offer. We charge the highest rates in our area, but that's because we offer the highest level of service. When talking to a client, we emphasize the elements I've described above, including the ease our AppFolio platform provides. We also mention that we're a corporate-backed company that is independently owned and operated, enabling us to offer the best of both worlds.

If you can offer a better service and clearly communicate a great value proposition, explaining, "Here are the ten things that I do, and I do them so well that they're worth that 10 percent fee or that one month's rent up front," then you shut down the competition.

You've got to beat them where you can, because if it's just about price point, you'll never win—especially if your rates are the highest in the area. Remember, too, that it's not worth your time to deal with owners who only care about a base price, as they make difficult clients. Instead, you want clients who will understand that those rates reflect the level of service and attention to detail you provide.

The key is knowing what you do better than everyone else, along with your competitors' shortfalls, and communicating both to prospective clients.

The other point to make is that you can provide these quality services precisely *because* you charge the homeowner enough to pay for them. Make it clear that if you lowered your fees, you would have to sacrifice some of the services you offer.

When you think about it, what's your time worth? If you're getting 6 or 7 percent from people, you'll be spread too thin. You won't be able to hire enough people to backfill the positions that you need. Other companies take smaller percentages than we do, but they don't have enough people and, as a result, they don't have the information they need if they find themselves facing a dispute. Don't devalue yourself in pursuit of market share. Know what you're worth. Know what you need to charge to build your company, and communicate the why behind your rates.

Key Insights

- In general, the same marketing tools and strategies that work for you in sales will also benefit your property management business.

- Plan a launch. Tell everyone in your sphere that you will be entering the property management space.

- To reach multiunit property owners, cultivate relationships with their gatekeepers: lawyers, CPAs, and financial advisors.

- The typical owner of an investment property is older and will respond well to print media, including direct mail and ads in local business newspapers and magazines.

- Don't underestimate the power of the old-fashioned telephone. Call multiunit owners and ask them if they are happy with their present property management company.

- Approach owners of mom-and-pop property management

companies. Many of these people are elderly and have grown tired of their management duties. That paves the way for you to earn their business.

- Potential clients respond positively to above-and-beyond property management services, such as fast pay, professional photos, MLS listings, and airtight move-in/move-out policies.

- Find ways to solicit a multitude of good reviews. At the same time, have a policy in place for dealing with negative reviews.

- Don't be afraid to get creative when sourcing new clients. For instance, responding to RFPs can help you acquire student properties and other housing projects financed by local and state economic-development agencies.

- Market to expired listings. Explain that you can list the property as a rental and/or a sale.

- When marketing to potential first-time investors, acknowledge that most owners dislike managing properties.

- Become an expert in your market. Learn to use the financial formulas by which investors measure profit potential. And finally, don't hesitate to highlight your value proposition.

CHAPTER 8

GET YOUR OPERATIONS IN ORDER

Let's turn our attention to operations, and the ways in which many of the elements of property management we discussed come together in your business—both in your day-to-day activities and on a larger scale. Just as with marketing, in many cases, it's about maintaining consistency and establishing policies and processes that address those pain points.

Our director of operations, Shane Snoots, is one of the best in the business. He holds the record for the most properties leased in a single year at Long & Foster—204—and he has helped us onboard more than twelve hundred accounts. He's also been by my side from the beginning. Together we've established and adapted effective systems that promote day-to-day and big picture success.

With that in mind, it's important to note that Rome wasn't built in a day, and neither was our property management business. So let's talk about our timeline.

A Timeline for Growth

Over time, our model, policies, and processes have expanded alongside our growing business. When we first started, Shane, Tasha (our accounting director), and I were the only three employees in our business—forming the three legs of the stool we discussed in our hiring chapter (you'll remember that I handled business development, and Shane tackled maintenance).

When we hit three or four hundred accounts, we all felt as if we had reached our maximum capacity and agreed that we would benefit from a full-time maintenance coordinator—that became our next hire.

At five or six hundred accounts, we found ourselves looking for leasing agents to help manage the influx, as well as someone to conduct inspections full time—a task that our maintenance coordinator had been handling previously.

Somewhere between six hundred and eight hundred accounts, Shane suggested hiring an inside sales agent (ISA) to handle all the leads that were coming our way.

Why is an ISA a helpful addition to your team once things start to pick up and you have the resources to do so? When you do your marketing right, you'll find yourself with a lot of leads. That means you'll need a process—and perhaps an individual or two—to handle them. For instance, we've had seventeen hundred new leasing leads come in during the last thirty days. That's a lot of leads, and—since we've covered the importance of consistency—you've probably guessed that we don't respond with just one phone call. Our ISA will make three or four calls to each lead. If the lead doesn't answer the phone after we've tried four times, that lead is dead to us, and we move on. We assume that the person has already found a place to live.

In our business, our ISA's support has been a huge benefit—making it possible for us to rent at the rate that we do (we're filling thirty to forty properties a month on average).

With someone to make calls to prospective renters from sunup to sundown, Shane has the time to talk with our homeowners, nurturing those relationships and ensuring every client we serve has what they need—including the support to purchase new properties.

People expect and deserve a high level of service, and it's part of the value proposition we offer them during our early conversations. But each person on our team can only divide their time in so many different ways. Let's say Shane is tasked with managing all of our operations and chasing down leads. He may be rushed on a phone call, wrapping things up in just two minutes because he only *has* two minutes before he has to tend to his next task. But the ISA has all the time in the world to provide the level of service we've promised and focus on the details.

That's also a major benefit when Shane heads out to meet a potential renter. The ISA has already equipped him with all the information he needs—and spent time walking the renter through the application process. That way, if the renter is interested in moving forward, we're all set up for a seamless transaction.

Now, I know that property management is a skinny business. Right out of the box, a company just won't have the capacity to hire six or seven people—the income won't be there. That's why, for example, the ISA role didn't come about until we had filled those key hiring positions in accounting, business development, and maintenance and were able to backfill. Once they were all set, and we had the capacity to hire an ISA and some leasing agents, we were able to go into full growth mode, and Shane was able to turn his focus from just putting people in the houses we managed to actually going out and getting houses for prospective tenants.

This isn't to say our timeline should be yours. My goal here is to share our basic trajectory, complete with the benchmarks and milestones that informed our process. That way, you can anticipate the moments in your growth process that may require an operational shift.

Your market may also be different from ours, and that may bring about a different set of benchmarks. For example, in Southern California, New Jersey, or New York, where rents are much higher, you may be working a different set of numbers, as your income on each account will be higher.

You may also find a different staffing pathway that works for you. For example, if you're starting out with a limited budget, you may want to consider bringing on a virtual assistant as a maintenance coordinator. With the capacity to work forty hours a week, it's the next best thing to making your own hire. While you have to be very descriptive about what you're asking them to do, you can select a property management assistant who will understand your platform at an extremely affordable rate. Plus, if your virtual assistant does leave for some reason, their company will provide a replacement right away and conduct any necessary training; it's just up to you to provide specifics about how you want things done.

> *Ultimately, you have to learn when to move the needle in a manner that works for your business and your market.*

Ultimately, you have to learn when to move the needle in a

manner that works for your business and your market. That's how you avoid burnout, ensure smooth operations, and carve out a path for growth.

Managing the Day-to-Day Hustle

What does day-to-day operations management look like in a successful property management business? Shane shared the schedule and habits that keep him—and our organization—on track.

Even though he's been with us since the beginning, he still maintains the old school mentality of "be the first one in the office, and the last one to leave." Getting there early—around 7:00 a.m.—enables him to get all his paperwork done before the phone starts ringing. After 9:00 a.m., he explained, "I always say I'm pissing on fires."

From 9:00 a.m. to 5:00 p.m., it's those fires, appointments, talking with new homeowners, or discussing our marketing plan with the marketing director. Managing his time also requires taking into account where he must go. Sometimes, that means driving to Delaware or across the state of Maryland, since we cover such a large region. But the day doesn't end there. Often, he's back at it until 6:30 p.m., addressing the administrative items he didn't have a chance to tackle during the day.

For him, success is all about structuring his day—knowing that, from 7:00 a.m. until 9:00 a.m., he'll be working on nothing but leases, new property management agreements, and new listings; that the typical nine-to-five workday will be a whirlwind; and that the last hour and a half or so is set aside for administrative tasks.

To get a handle on it all, he keeps it old school as well. Each morning, he writes the activities for the day on a yellow legal pad and crosses them off as he finishes them. If there are items left from the day before, he tackles those first. Whether or not you follow Shane's personal operations strategy to a T, writing things down—whether with paper and pen or on a device—is essential to capture the intricacies of the role. For example, the leasing process requires numerous steps, from inspection and cleaning to move-in day. A thorough list can help ensure nothing accidentally falls off your plate.

Another key tip? Make time for a mental break at some point during the day, even if it means putting in an hour or two at a different time. Shane also makes sure to focus on the task at hand, so when he's handling paperwork, he turns his phone off or sets it aside so that he won't be interrupted.

Once the business had more resources, we were also able to adjust some day-to-day processes. We got someone to help Shane with a portion of the paperwork and leases and switched over to a voice over IP (VoIP) system, which routes callers to whomever they need to reach so the whole office wasn't getting crushed by phone calls—especially ones that may have been misdirected in the first place. When we began taking calls on a limited number of topics, and filtering all others through the AppFolio system, we found ourselves fielding hundreds less calls a day. That upped our efficiency significantly.

It's also important to maintain the phone policies you've instated. Sometimes, people on your team build relationships with tenants. Because they have an existing relationship, when a maintenance issue arises, they'll call that person directly rather than contacting the maintenance line. To counter that, we give all our tenants a packet at move-in time that lists the various phone numbers and procedures they may need, including a maintenance line, an emergency line, and key checklists. And when they do contact someone directly, we make sure to guide them to the appropriate channel—even if it seems like it would be faster to call the maintenance line or put in the work order ourselves. Why? If we do them a favor once, they'll reach out for personal assistance time and again.

There's another risk that we avoid with this policy: that tenants might say, "I talked to someone from your office about a problem. Don't you have a record of it?" That situation puts us in a potentially dangerous position, one that proper fielding and documentation avoids. Trust me, you don't want to have to look back through all your text messages ten months after the fact to prove that you told a tenant one thing, when they insist that you said another.

To be efficient and grow, you have to stay true to those systems and processes. We also made sure each person had an individual role to play, and that they knew what that role was—a distinction that has helped everyone we employ determine their day-to-day activities. There's no value in having a jack of all trades on your team. Each player should be the best at their specific role. They should be answering all of *their* calls to the best of their ability, not fielding ones for other roles in the organization.

What's Most Important

What's the best advice Shane has to offer when you're just starting out in property management?

Know your players—who's on your team—and the roles each of them needs to fill. We didn't have a map to get where we are today, but at the outset, Shane dissected the role of a property manager. He

> Know your players—who's on your team—and the roles each of them needs to fill.

made sure he understood each aspect of it, determined our strengths and weaknesses, and subsequently created positions to bolster those weak areas. And when he doled out specific responsibilities, he made sure that person knew they should be focused entirely on the tasks assigned to them—and nothing else.

We learned early on that property managers wore many different hats—often too many to get a job done well—and that most companies hadn't done the work to separate skill sets. In fact, when we look back on our early days, one reason we were able to gain market share was because our competitors were wearing too many hats and performing tasks that they weren't good at. The bottom line is that you shouldn't be afraid to break down every element of your business, and ensure you have the talent, policies, and processes to make things work.

When it comes to efficiency, you should also consider your inspection process. Inspections eat time. They can take between thirty and sixty minutes each, depending on the size of the house and the type of inspection being done—plus any travel time necessary to reach the property. Don't forget to factor that in when you're doling out responsibilities or tending to your daily task list.

Another essential factor in building a successful property management business? Find good, reliable contractors. When we first started, we often hired fly-by-night individuals because we didn't know any better. After getting burned a few times, we built a preferred vendor program, leveraging our book of business to get better service and better pricing for our homeowners. That's crucial, because the quality of the maintenance work done by those you hire reflects on you. Today, tenants and landlords alike frequently call us to share what a great experience they've had with a particular electrician or plumber. Those we work with have become an extension of our team. And when owners purchase homes right out of foreclosure with numerous issues that need fixing, they reach out for our help.

To meet the various needs that will arise at different properties over time, you must have a full slate of vendors whom you trust and to whom you can reach out in an emergency. If you don't have a general contractor, an electrician, and a plumber—for starters—you're dead in the water.

Finally, as we discussed in the previous chapter, know your competitors. That's what drives our operations—and our business as a whole—every day. We want to be better than everyone else, to be the best at what we do. Go into this business asking, "How can I improve the level of service in my market?" and then take steps to operationalize everything you identify. Remember, people are waiting for good service. And when you can provide it, your partnership becomes priceless.

Key Insights

- Consider your growth timeline and identify when you may need more help to cover day-to-day responsibilities.

- Be organized and follow a daily routine that maximizes your efficiency. Set specific times for addressing paperwork.

- Make time for mental breaks. You'll be handling a lot, and taking a few moments to breathe can help you keep it all in perspective and under control.

- Ensure everyone has their own role, with specific tasks, and make sure they know what their responsibilities are to be as effective as possible.

- A VoIP system can help you avoid the crush of calls and be way more efficient.

- Use AppFolio or a similar program to receive, document, and track maintenance calls. Never take maintenance calls in your office. Insist that your tenants follow proper procedures.

- Having too few employees will limit your efficiency and growth. An inside sales agent may be a helpful addition to your team down the line, after you've filled the pressing positions we discussed in our hiring chapter.

- If you can't afford to hire a full-time maintenance coordinator early on, bringing on a property management virtual assistant may be a major boon to your business—at an extremely affordable rate.

- Find good, reliable contractors. The vendors you hire are a reflection of your company.

- Resolve to provide the best service in your market.

CHAPTER 9

THE MOVE-IN/MOVE-OUT PROCESS

Picture this: you arrive for a move-out inspection at a home you manage. As a seasoned property manager, you've seen it all, but you still get a bit nervous going into these. You're never quite sure what to expect. You unlock the front door, step inside ... and breathe a sigh of relief. The floors are gleaming. The window screens and shades are intact. Walking through the bedrooms, you can see that the carpets have been steam cleaned, as requested. Even the fridge is completely spotless. Every direction you've given the exiting tenants has been followed to a T.

Of course, there's always the flip side. That door cracks open, and you're hit with an awful but hard-to-place smell. Is it garbage? Cat urine? The walls are pockmarked with holes, and the blinds are coated in a thick layer of dust and broken in some places. The carpets are marked with mysterious stains. Getting the property back online will take more than a little elbow grease. And the reality is you've got to be prepared to handle both situations—and account for everything that's happened to the property since that first move-in inspection.

Now that we've begun unpacking the details of what it takes to run a successful property management business, we must talk about the move-in/move-out process. Handle it well, and you will have the evidence necessary to defend your company against most disputes brought by a landlord or tenant. Miss a few items in your inspections, leave holes in your documentation, or violate any state regulations pertaining to security deposits and you could find yourself in court facing significant costs. Because, chances are, even those who have wrecked the place in a manner that seems beyond obvious will inquire as to why they're not getting that security deposit back.

> **Documenting everything keeps you covered, especially if you find yourself called to present evidence in front of a judge.**

And without evidence, you may be out of luck. Why? I'm not aware of any clear, concise definition of what normal wear and tear looks like—making it a tremendous gray area when it comes to security deposits. Documenting everything keeps you covered, especially if you find yourself called to present evidence in front of a judge.

In this chapter, we'll offer critical advice concerning security deposits, and we'll discuss best practices for conducting "dispute-proof" move-in/move-out inspections. Put them in place now, and thank me later.

Your Fourth Hire

First, think about who will take care of this aspect of your operation. The move-in/move-out process leaves little to no room for error. You simply can't allow any of the tasks associated with the process to "fall through the cracks." After all, the penalties for missteps can be major. My recommendation: as soon as your finances will allow, hire a diligent, detail-oriented individual to manage the process for you. They can then coordinate with your maintenance coordinator, who will be busy holding down the fort and directing calls and contractors at the office. Having an inspection team ensures everyone can attend to their role properly and in a timely manner, without missing any steps along the way.

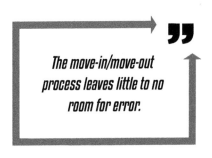

The move-in/move-out process leaves little to no room for error.

Though most situations they'll encounter won't be too extreme, it can also be helpful to have a strong stomach alongside a healthy dose of grit. And while a diligent, detail-oriented approach is a must, keep in mind that you can train someone on how to conduct each process. However, experience in the field helps. We hired an individual with a background in contracting, which has been quite helpful when it comes to inspections.

Having an individual or team who can conduct inspections ASAP has saved us numerous times. Just recently, for instance, our team conducted a move-out inspection on a property that had been left in great condition. When they returned a few days later, they found a water leak that had been running for twenty-four hours or so. It had caused significant damage in that short time. But without designated individuals to follow up and address issues like these, things would have been much worse. The same is true for another wild circumstance we encountered: upon arriving at a home for a move-out inspection, one of our staff members found that the tenant had left behind a litter of kittens!

This hire can also help institute and maintain the conveyer belt–like efficiency that's essential to smooth operations. You can see why it's worthwhile to bring them on board as soon as you can.

Security Deposits

As you likely know by now, if a storm brews between tenant and landlord, it will most likely swirl around the issue of security deposits—98 percent of the time we've found ourselves in court, it's due to a security deposit issue. The landlord will claim that the tenant owes for damages, and the tenant will dispute the amount, or perhaps claim to owe nothing at all. Meanwhile, even though your company's property management agreement may state that such conflicts shall exist solely between the tenant and the landlord, you may nevertheless find yourself in court, either as a named defendant or as a witness.

How can you forestall, or at least mitigate, such troubles? Consider the advice below, which my team has gleaned from personal experience.

Study and obey the laws and regulations that govern security deposits in your state. Expect to follow rules that require you to:

- Place security deposits in escrow and pay interest at a predetermined minimum rate

- Provide former tenants with copies of bills paid to repair damage (when damage charges are deducted from the security deposit)

- Refund security money to the tenant within a limited time period or pay heavy fines

- Limit the tenant's responsibilities for damage (state laws may dictate what your lease can and cannot list as tenant responsibilities)

Create an airtight system for conducting and documenting move-in and move-out inspections. We follow a strict inspection process, and we document everything in writing. I'll talk more about our process in a moment, but the goal here is to have ample evidence when tenants or landlords raise questions about new or existing damage.

Practice strict accounting. Be prepared to produce records of all transactions related to the property, including interest earned on security deposits.

When taking on a property previously managed by the landlord, insist that you keep the security deposit. By doing so, you can be certain that the deposit will be managed and distributed properly.

Document all interactions with the landlord, tenant, and contractors. A powerful software program will track and store these interactions automatically.

Be aware that a misstep can produce substantial liabilities. Be diligent, be organized, and follow your established processes in accordance with state law.

The Move-In Process

Having covered the steps to take when it comes to security deposits, let's consider the move-in process. There are two elements here: the move-in inspection and the tenant's responsibilities.

Naturally, we inspect the property thoroughly before a new tenant takes possession of it. We check *and document in writing* the condition of *everything*. We inspect the rooms, the closets, the floors, the doors, and the windows (including any screens, shades, or blinds). We open the cabinets and drawers. We run all the water and all the appliances to make sure they're functioning properly. We note the condition of the building's exterior and, if applicable, the grounds. (For additional evidence, we may take as many as three hundred photos.) We then communicate our findings to the landlord, and, if repairs are needed, we offer to make those repairs.

Once the house is ready for occupancy, we focus on the tenant's responsibilities. Before we allow the person to move in, we require proof that they have obtained renter's insurance and placed all utilities in their name (to the extent allowed by state law). After the renter takes possession, we give the person fifteen days to complete a tenant's move-in inspection.

The Move-Out Process

When it comes time for the tenant to move out, the process flips. We first address the tenant's responsibilities and then conduct a move-out inspection. To begin with, we require the departing renter to complete a number of tasks, which we specify for them on a checklist. Among the items to complete, we stipulate that the tenant must pay to have the home professionally cleaned—this includes having the carpets steam cleaned.

The tenant must also accomplish certain tasks before they become eligible to receive a full or partial refund of the security deposit. That includes having the space professionally cleaned, returning keys on time, and leaving gas or oil tanks filled to the level they were at when the tenants moved in. We also let the person know that deadlines apply.

We are also careful not to begin any repairs or upgrades to a property until after we have completed the move-out inspection, as those findings might change our approach. For example, if we find major structural damage, that will have to be taken care of before we bring in someone to paint the walls.

Once the home is empty, we conduct a detailed move-out inspection, documenting our findings in writing, taking photos, and carefully noting any damage. Just as with the move-in process, we examine everything. Next, we save our inspection findings directly into AppFolio. Whether you record your information on paper or in computer files, be sure to create copies or backups. Your data is simply too important to lose; without it, you could be in serious trouble if a dispute were to arise.

While we've never lost any important data—thankfully— switching from one software system to another and managing the significant challenge of ensuring all the information transferred over emphasized for us just how important it is to keep tabs on all that information.

We then report our findings to the owner, including cost estimates for repairing any damage. Although the owner will often ask us to suggest how much money they should withhold in total from the security deposit, we make it clear that it is their responsibility (*not ours!*) to determine that figure.

Next, observing state-mandated protocols and deadlines, we return the remainder of the security deposit to the former tenant. (Be careful; penalties for missteps can be severe. Here in Maryland, fines can reach triple the amount of the security deposit.)

Landlord-Management Disagreements

Unfortunately, we've worked with many landlords who wanted to charge a former tenant for damage that clearly existed before the tenant moved in. Since you will encounter this problem sooner or later, you should be proactive and create a process for dealing with it. In our case, we advise the landlord in writing of our opinion about the damage, noting that we have based our conclusions on evidence gathered during our inspections. We further advise that the landlord must indemnify our company against any potential liability and that, if the tenant sues the landlord, we will not be held responsible.

We've encountered numerous situations in which the landlord decides to unlawfully charge tenants for damage, only to lose in court. In those cases, our records serve as crucial evidence for the judge—and protect us to boot. On the flip side, we've had tenants dispute the decision to keep our security deposit, which also acts as evidence. Tenants fight you on it as well. That's why you need to have a record of everything.

Worth Repeating

I can't overemphasize the importance of some of the advice you've read here. These three tips should be top of mind as you establish your policies and procedures:

- Develop an airtight process for conducting move-in and move-out inspections. Document your findings in writing. (Remember, "If it's not in writing, it doesn't exist.")

- Understand and follow state laws that govern security deposits. Observe mandated timelines. When you don't, you risk significant penalties.

- Follow sound accounting practices. You should always have a paper trail in place. For example, keep contractor bills that corroborate any repair costs deducted from security deposits. You'll want to be able to pull them easily if the charges are ever called into question.

Key Insights

- No area of property management carries more liability for the property manager than the move-in/move-out process.

- As such, as soon as it's financially possible, hire someone to manage your move-in/move-out process.

- Most disputes involve security deposits.

- Know and diligently follow your state's laws and regulations pertaining to security deposits. Be aware of deadlines and potential fines.

- Follow sound accounting practices. Be prepared to produce records of all transactions related to a property, particularly receipts proving the cost of repairing damages caused by a tenant.

- Create an airtight process for inspecting properties. Take photos and document your findings in writing.

- Before allowing a tenant to move in, require proof that they have obtained renter's insurance and established utility accounts in their name.

- After move-in, require the tenant to conduct a move-in inspection.

- Devise a process for dealing with landlord and tenant disputes when it comes to the security deposit.

- Don't risk losing important inspection data. Copy it or back it up.

CHAPTER 10

BUILDING ANCILLARY BUSINESSES

We've talked about all the benefits a property management business can provide, despite—or rather, due to—all the hard work involved. But the opportunity for growth and success doesn't stop there. Beyond generating management and leasing fees, your property management business will offer you many chances to build new, ancillary silos of income. And it gets better: by creating property management-related side ventures, which you might own entirely or participate in jointly with other businesspeople, you can improve your customer service and more than double the income your business brings in. We have entered into these relationships several times, in virtually every industry associated with property management, and across a number of different models. When done well, they can be one of the most lucrative aspects of this business.

Here, we'll break down some of the opportunities available to you—and how to play your cards right if you choose to pursue them.

Don't Overlook Compliance

First, however, a few words of caution. Before expanding into any new business venture, consult with an attorney to make sure that your planned activities will comply with the Real Estate Settlement Procedures Act (RESPA), a federal consumer protection law that dictates the disclosures that must be made to help homebuyers make informed decisions, and any other applicable laws to ensure compliance. Once you determine that your plans will pass muster, hire the attorney to draw up any necessary documents, including your affiliated-business disclosures, which should be specific to your intended operations. Also make certain that your agreements will limit your liability should disputes, injuries, or other problems occur.

Next, talk to your CPA about your future federal and state tax obligations, including workman's compensation and other payroll taxes. Just as with your property management business, crossing your t's and dotting your i's from the get-go will help you launch and sustain an efficient and successful operation.

Insurance

Consider filling your first tall silo with insurance dollars. As your property management business grows, you can make substantial income providing policies to your landlords and tenants (not to mention your sales clients). An easy way to jump into the insurance game is to arrange a joint venture or a marketing partnership with an existing company. A more ambitious plan would be to open your own firm. Either way, if you offer convenience and a good, competitively priced product, you will create a new and reliable income source from your pool of existing clients.

Contractors

What do painters, roofers, plumbers, HVAC techs, carpenters, landscapers, electricians, and cleaning crews have in common? They are all contractors whom you will rely upon *every day* when your properties need attention. So wouldn't it make sense to employ these good people yourself or, alternatively, to forge some sort of mutually beneficial business alliance with them?

There are three ways to align yourself with contractors, and I've tried all of them:

- Under Plan *A*, you own and operate your own contracting businesses, and the workers are your employees.

- Under Plan *B*, you create a joint venture with existing businesses.

Which plan would work best for you? That depends on the extent and nature of your infrastructure; what you have the wherewithal to do financially; what profit margins your market will allow; and, above all, the level of commitment that you are willing to make to the venture.

Full-scale ownership offers you complete control over your services and promises high profits, supported primarily by your property management accounts. You'll also experience all the challenges (and headaches) of running one or more new businesses, so it's worth weighing whether that's something you want to take on.

Meanwhile, a complementary joint venture typically allows the contractor to focus on what they do best while you, the partner, contribute back-end services and business systems that the contractor lacks. This arrangement, which might involve revenue sharing or some sort of fee system, can prove lucrative for both parties.

A referral arrangement generates modest (but welcome) sums of "mailbox money" while demanding very little of your time.

Essential Steps

Regardless of how you choose to approach contracting, put these two items near the top of your to-do list:

First, if you are to make money, you must know prices in your market. You cannot price your services above the market. The relationships you form should help you stay on target and even offer discounts, creating a better deal for everyone. To determine pricing, we researched the cost of the average service call in various areas and aimed to price our services 5 percent lower than that.

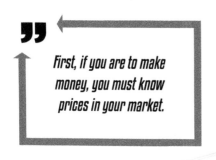

First, if you are to make money, you must know prices in your market.

That would allow us to be a little cheaper than the rest of the market, without shorting our contractors or sacrificing quality.

Second, whether you own, partially own, or otherwise associate yourself with a business that will potentially serve a landlord, you must fully disclose your interests. Go beyond presenting the landlord with your affiliated-business disclosure form. Sit down with them, have a conversation, and position your interest in the side business as a benefit. Stress that your connection to the business will promote efficiency, savings, and superior customer service.

They should understand that these affiliations only strengthen your value proposition.

What Will You Bring to the Table?

Of course, it's not just about what others can do for you; the ways in which you can contribute to another venture are just as important. Over the years, we determined that the joint-venture model works best for us. We now have joint ventures covering general construction, HVAC, plumbing—really everything related to maintaining a property.

In forging our alliances, we looked for ways that our company, with its particular strengths and resources, could support the needs of our partners. One thing we learned is that contractors may be very good at what they do in the field, but they often struggle to manage their back-end activities. Thus, we proposed taking over those back-end chores for them so that they could focus on their on-site work. When you pursue a joint venture, suggest services that you can perform for your potential partner; don't simply promise to fill the person's appointment schedule.

Helping (and Profiting) in Other Ways

Any time you can help your partner operate more efficiently, you also help yourself. Here are three ways in which we support our contractors and, at the same time, make additional income for ourselves.

Any time you can help your partner operate more efficiently, you also help yourself.

1. **Fronting the costs of materials.** Many contractors experience cash-flow problems, often because they need to purchase expensive materials before they can begin a job. We solved that problem by, first, opening "pro accounts" with Lowe's, The Home Depot, and our largest suppliers; and second, by allowing our partner contractors to carry the materials from the stores under our name—without having to lay out cash. The contractors appreciate our fronting the costs and let us charge a markup on the goods when we invoice the client, or split the profit of a markup with us when that client payment comes through. Because we go through so many materials in a year, those markups add up for us.

2. **Buying in bulk.** In a typical year, we purchase vast amounts of flooring, paint, appliances, smoke detectors, and other residential necessities. By buying in bulk and at deep discounts, we are able to offer below-wholesale discounts to our contractors and still make a margin for ourselves. I should note also that very often the contractors are able to pass along a portion of their savings to the landlords, so everyone benefits.

3. **We pay quickly.** We pay all of our contractors (affiliated or not) every Friday, so they don't have to endure the uncertainty of waiting for a net-thirty or net-sixty check to arrive. Because they appreciate our policy—and because we're able to send them so much business—many contractors are willing to work for us for a little less money than what they would normally charge. We've also noticed that these happy contractors respond more quickly to our service calls. It's yet another helpful service that enables everyone to win.

A Tale of Cool Savings

File this story under "Volume Discounts." We manage a huge, older apartment complex that, a while back, needed some renovations. We went to an HVAC manufacturer and said, "Hey, over the next two years, we're going to buy a hundred units from you. How much will you discount them? And we're willing to sign a contract."

The response was better than we expected. We were able to purchase the units for almost 60 percent less than what any local vendor would have charged. As a result, we could charge a good markup and still provide the units to the owner of the complex at a price that was lower than retail. It was a good deal for the apartment owner and an extremely lucrative deal for us.

The moral of the story: as your accounts multiply, you and your maintenance coordinator should look at the materials that you consume in high volume and ask yourselves, "How can we purchase these things cheaply in bulk?"

As an aside, I'll add that very often the supplier will store the materials for you for a period of time so that you won't even need to take possession of them. The contractors can pick up the items as needed, and all you'll have to do is bill them accordingly and make your profit.

Hefty Numbers

When your property management business grows to several hundred accounts, you will probably bill in excess of $1.5 million annually in maintenance costs. If your markups and fees yield 20 percent of that figure, your profit will be $300,000—money that will go right to your bottom line. (Do you see that we're talking about big dollars here?)

We've also found other ways to nourish our bottom line. Many times suppliers will offer rebates if you purchase enough product to reach some predetermined metric. If you hit one of those milestones and save 2 or 3 percent on a large-volume purchase, you earn pass-through dollars that result as a by-product of your company's growth. When earned repeatedly, rebates of even small percentages can add up to very large sums.

Another way to earn discounts from suppliers is to develop relationships with them and tell them that you'd be interested in any special deals that might come along. We've told suppliers, "Hey, when you guys are having a huge sale or you've got to move product, we're interested in buying what you have."

In fact, there have been many times when a vendor was planning to discontinue a line of flooring or appliances, for example, and we were able to grab that product for a bargain price. The lesson here: as your company grows and you start to use a lot of materials, look for ways to buy in bulk. Think big. There have been times when we bought $40,000 or $50,000 worth of material for 60 to 70 percent off retail prices. We marked it up, made a good margin, and were still able to offer the products to our consumers at a discount.

One more option as to how you can push extra dollars to your bottom line? A cash-back credit card. Most of the time, we buy our materials on a cash-back credit card. If we collect rebates of 3 to 4 percent on, say, $400,000 worth of goods, we earn bonus dollars in the neighborhood of $16,000! That's major—and it's essentially free money.

So Many Opportunities

If you create ancillary businesses or business alliances and then look for opportunities to save money on the goods and services you repeatedly purchase, you can turn your property management business into an extremely lucrative enterprise. In fact, your "ancillary money" may easily top the revenue you make from management fees.

I can't stress this point enough: from the very beginning, build these income silos into your business plan. Those silos will fill with cash at faster and faster rates as your management accounts increase.

Meanwhile, Over on the Sales Side

Here's another bonus benefit that you should consider. Whatever a contractor can do for your landlords and tenants, they can also do for a buyer or seller. If a buyer starts to back away from purchasing a property that has a nasty punch list, you can say, "No problem. I'll have one of my guys from property management do the repairs for you." If a seller needs to freshen up a house before listing it, you can say, "My contractors can handle any job, large or small. I'll have them contact you."

You'll offer a higher level of customer service, you'll solve the client's problems, and you'll make additional profit.

Today, we're involved in businesses related to every service we offer—from landscaping and flooring to building houses. And those investments have paid off in spades.

Key Insights

- Your property management business will offer you many opportunities to create lucrative side ventures.

- Consult your attorney to make certain that your proposed activities will comply with RESPA and all other applicable laws. Visit your CPA to ask about workman's compensation and other payroll taxes.

- Consider selling insurance to your landlords, tenants, and sales clients.

- Build your own contracting businesses or align yourself with established contracting firms. Either way, you will create lucrative income streams supported primarily by your existing property management clients.

- Disclose your business alliances to your landlords and highlight them as a real benefit, stressing that your partnerships will enable you to provide better customer service.

- When possible, buy materials in bulk and at deep discounts. Often you will be able to sell the items to your contractors at below-retail prices while still making a healthy spread for yourself.

- Tell your suppliers that you might be willing to help them out when they need to move discontinued product.

- Find ways to please your contractor partners. Pay them weekly and front the costs of their materials. In return, they will treat you well.

- Open "pro accounts" with Lowe's, The Home Depot, and other suppliers. Charge large purchases on a cash-back card to rack up free money.

- A property management business with several hundred accounts may bill $1.5 million in annual maintenance charges. If you keep 20 percent of that sum in fees and markups, you will send $300,000 in profit to your bottom line.

- Having relationships with a variety of contractors will support the sales side of your business as well, allowing you to better serve your buyers and sellers.

CONCLUSION

We've covered the major opportunities—and challenges—that lie in launching and sustaining a property management business. If you're looking for a strong residual income provider and you're ready and willing to handle the inevitable hurdles that will come your way, it's a great way to build wealth.

Our property management business has helped me build a sizeable net worth and significant assets in real estate. Today, I own nearly five hundred properties on my own, a majority of which have come to me through property management. It has helped me establish one of the most influential platforms in our industry. And importantly, it's an excellent complement to my other business ventures, especially real estate sales.

As of this writing, our parent company, Long & Foster, is in nine states and has two hundred offices in the District of Columbia. It was the number one independent brokerage in the world until Warren Buffett bought it a couple years ago. My real estate team was number one in home sales for the entire company, number one in the state of Maryland for home sales this year, and number five in the country. Our property management business has contributed to and bolstered that success and fueled our growth.

Don't hesitate to think big.

If you're intrigued by that concept, don't be afraid to go after it. And don't hesitate to think big. There's so much opportunity in property management. You're looking at a landscape run by small mom-and-pop shops and huge institutions, with little in between—and plenty of room for disruption. You have the opportunity to take a permanent market share, particularly since so many are deterred by the work inherent in the job.

Couple that with the opportunities that property management presents when it comes to investing in real estate, which helps you grow your wealth by sheltering taxes and amass major equity—not to mention opportunities for ancillary businesses—and you have an incredible value proposition that will continue to feed your sales business and vice versa.

With that said, to thrive in this market, you have to meet consumer expectations. In a world dominated by companies that have determined how to solve a slew of problems—and to do it now, like Amazon, Apple, and Uber—you have to meet the expectations they have cultivated. In fact, they're your competition—not others in the real estate industry.

When you can meet every need a customer may have, from mortgages to titles, property management, insurance, and home renovations—in the most convenient manner possible—you become the

Amazon of realty. And those who do will dominate our market going forward. Meanwhile, those who don't will be left in the dust. If all you can do is help people buy and sell their homes, you're going to be in trouble.

Fortunately, in these pages, you have the information you need to do things differently. I wish you the best of luck—and the grit to make it happen.

FOR MORE TRAINING AND INFORMATION ON THIS COURSE VISIT BRANDONSBRAIN.ORG

Printed in the USA
CPSIA information can be obtained
at www.ICGtesting.com
JSHW012053140824
68134JS00035B/3420

9 781642 252668